DR. DARRELL PARSONS

Emerging as an Innovative Christian Leader

12 Common Cores for Mobilizing Your Influence into the Future

GLE Books
Stafford, Virginia USA

Emerging as an Innovative Leader—12 Common Cores for Mobilizing Your Influence into the Future
by Dr. Darrell J. Parsons

GLE Books
an imprint of Parsons Publishing House
P. O. Box 488
Stafford, VA 22555 USA
www.ParsonsPublishingHouse.com
Info@ParsonsPublishingHouse.com

Printed in the United States of America.
For World-Wide Distribution.

Trade Paper:
ISBN -13: 978-1-60273-065-6
ISBN -10: 160273-065-2
Library of Congress Control Number: 2015907140

Also available in Case Laminate Hardback:
ISBN -13: 978-1-60273-064-9
ISBN -10: 160273-064-4
Library of Congress Control Number: 2014918091

TABLE OF CONTENTS

Introduction

"If you always do what you always did,
you will always get what you always got."
—Albert Einstein

"Our wretched species is so made that those
who walk on the well-trodden path always
throw stones at those who are showing a new road."
—Voltaire

"Change is the law of life. And those who look only to the
past or present are certain to miss the future."
—John F. Kennedy

The value of an idea is a powerful thing, and the seed-bed for ideas is found in wisdom and understanding. Creating value ties wisdom and knowledge to innovation. According to Oster, the key to creating value in a specific product, service, idea, or process is innovation, which provides a steady stream of new products to businesses competing in a global marketplace (Oster, 2011, p. 16). Innovation may be the key to what many organizations will look like in the future.

Innovation can even save lives. Stop and think about some of the creative and innovative ideas of this modern era. Imagine Rip Van Wrinkle waking up in today's modern society of digital natives and real time information flow. However, innovation is not limited to modern societies with technological enhancements. Innovation can also exist in the deepest jungles and the most remote parts of the world. Ideas can change the world, or, as in Modupe's case, save the known world.

Modupe, whose name means "I am grateful", lived in a village in the deepest part of Africa, where the people made their living by farming. The village lay in a large green valley that was lined with palm trees and bushes. Surrounding the village were fields dotted with crops of yams, cassava, corn, and other vegetables. Just beyond the fields was a deep river that the villagers called Baba, which means father. The river was a friend and a provider for the people: the men used it for fishing, the women washed clothes on its banks, and the children played in its waters. But in the rainy season, the river overflowed, and the people were fearful of its power. So, at a place where the river wound beyond the fields, they built a strong dam to hold back the water.

> Modupe was a shy, quiet man whose wife had died and whose children were all married, so he had moved to the top of the mountain overlooking the valley and lived alone. There he had built a small hut and cleared a small piece of land to grow his vegetables. The people did not see Modupe often, but they loved and respected him because he had the gift of healing the sick and because he was one of them.
>
> One year at harvest time, there were unusually heavy rains, but the crops had done well, and there was much to do. No one paid it any mind. As Modupe stood by his home on the mountain, he noticed that the river had become swollen from the rains and was straining the dam. He knew that by the time he could run down to the village to warn the people of the flood, it would be too late and all would be lost. Even as Modupe watched, the wall of the dam began to break, and water started to seep through.
>
> Modupe thought of his friends in the village. Their crops, their homes, and their very lives were in danger if he did not find a way to warn them. Then an idea came to him: he rushed to his small hut and set it afire. When the people of the valley saw Modupe's house burning, they said, "Our friend is in trouble. Let's sound the alarm and go up to help him." Then, according to custom, men, women, and children ran up the mountain to see what they could do. When they reached

the top of the hill, they did not have time to ask what had happened—a loud crashing noise behind them made them turn around and look down into the valley. Their house, their temple, and their crops were being destroyed by the river, which had broken the dam and was flooding the valley.

The people began to cry and moan at their loss, but Modupe comforted them. "Don't worry," he said. "My crops are still here. We can share them while we build a new village." Then all the people began to sing and give thanks because they remembered that in coming to help a friend, they had saved themselves (Kouzes & Posner, 1993). Adapted from Nguzo Saba Films Teacher's Guide of film "Ujima" (San Francisco: Nguzo Saba Films) as reported in Friends Can Be Good Medicine (Sacremento, Calif.: California Department of Mental Health, 1981): 58-59.

The Laws of Change

Many times, ideas become the catalyst of change and change becomes the catalyst for innovation. Change is all around us. Seasons are constantly changing. Children are continuously growing and maturing. Relationships are always expanding. Even our bodies are constantly changing over time. Over 2500 years ago, Heraclitus recognized and concluded that nothing endures, but change. Change is everywhere, and the Laws of Change can be synthesized from the Laws of Thermodynamics.

The Thermodynamics of Change

Change requires an energy force in order for it to be lasting and beneficial. The First Law of Thermodynamics basically states that energy cannot be created or destroyed, but converted from one form to another. Therefore, the First Law of Change would be that change cannot be created or destroyed, but converted to work with you or against you. For example, shaping change can propel you into the future or anchor you to the past; wisdom comes in utilizing change to fulfill your purposes. The Second Law of Thermodynamics states that a system left to itself will tend to decay and become chaotic. The Second Law of Change would be that change must be reviewed and addressed or the organization will tend to decay and become obsolete. For example, a cutting-edge organization will sense the winds of change long before they are felt; whether in the product line or the administration of it, keeping up with the times is essential. The Third Law of Thermodynamics claims that all processes and movements cease as temperature approaches absolute zero. The paradox of this law is that absolute zero is not attainable. This would lead to the Third Law of Change which would state that change will only cease at absolute zero which cannot be achieved, so change is ever-present and always at work. Much like the Law of Gravity, change is ever-present and always at work regardless of the ability to see it.

Competition and Change

Competition is the very bedrock upon which we have built our free-market economy. While competition may be good for an external economic society, it is not always a good internal process for organizational change. Many organizations focus on some type of competitive reward program to create incentives for change or improvement. For example, the most sales this quarter wins a free trip. While this idea might sound good on the surface, competition inside an organization tends to isolate and drive people apart. Deming concludes that competition represents the forces of destruction that comes from the present style of reward for change found in most organizations today; whereas, a cooperative environment preserves the power of intrinsic motivation, dignity, innovative curiosity, and the joy of learning (Deming, 1994). Cooperation is a great enabler for success.

Cooperation and Change

Have you ever been caught in a rip current? The key to surviving a rip current that is pulling someone out to the ocean is not to resist and fight against the current, but to work with the current and swim parallel to the coast. Change, like rip currents, can quickly develop in an organization. To resist and compete against a rip current is to struggle against the odds and possibly even lose the battle. The swimmer must flow and work with the rip current and utilize that energy to be successful. Since the Laws of

Change identify that change is all around and constantly at work, the successful organization will work to use the energy of change to be successful rather than resist and compete against it. Cooperative change is about working with the current flow of change in order to produce a more effective and efficient organization. Innovation becomes a product of flowing with change as ideas surface throughout the organization.

The Key to Successful Change is Continuous Improvement

So, the question becomes how does a leader cooperate and use the energy of change for the good of the organization? The key to working with the continual process of change is to develop a mindset or a culture for continuous improvement. Competition only serves to drive people into isolation whereas cooperation is designed to bring people together. Noted author Dr. Stephen Covey identifies the principles of creative cooperation in his sixth habit of highly effective people, which is the habit of synergy (Covey, 1989). Buckminster Fuller, neo-futuristic architect and systems theorist, refined the definition of synergy to mean that the sum of the total is greater than the individual components (Fuller, 1975, p. 102). Simply stated, working together is better than working against or apart. The culture of continuous improvement allows everyone in the organization to work together to manage the energy of change for the good of the organization allowing innovation to surface. For example, in Washington DC, the Pentagon employs close to 24,000 people and has implemented a new security program utilizing those 24,000 pairs of eyes called, *"If You See Something—Say Something."* The strength of incorporating 24,000 people into a security conscious program is incredible. Everyone has ownership of this process and has readily adopted this new program change of heightened alert.

Kaizen

The concept of continuous improvement is not a new idea. It has been around for many years with success stories from around the globe. The Kaizen Institute at *http://us.kaizen.com* is one of many organizations promoting and teaching the concept of continuous improvement. ***Kaizen*** is a Japanese word that means "improvement" or "change for the better" and refers to the philosophy that focuses upon the continuous improvement of processes in manufacturing, engineering, game development, and business management. It has been applied in healthcare, psychotherapy, life-coaching, government, banking, and other industries. When used in the business sense and applied to the workplace, ***kaizen*** refers to activities that continually improve all functions, and involves all employees from the CEO to the assembly line workers.

This is not a top-down program. Bennis concludes that the idea of all successful change originating from top-down leadership is wrong, unrealistic, and maladaptive as well as potentially dangerous because it is based on the myth of the triumphant individual (Bennis, 2000). Kaizen is a cooperative program that is based upon the concept of continuous improvement. The Toyota Motor Corporation implemented the doctrine of kaizen or continuous improvement for every employee and applies it relentlessly as well as liberally across the corporation. One example is that Toyota offers a cash bonus to employees that can solve production glitches and one particular solved glitch resulted in slashing 75% of the cost of retrofitting the production line, which has saves billions of dollars annually (Daft, 2007).

No Man is an Island

As John Donne said, "No man is an island, entire of itself; every man is a piece of the continent, a part of the main." Transitioning from a competitive environment to a cooperative environment empowers people to take ownership of the change process and allows their gifts and talents to become vital assets to corporate worth. Dr. Bruce Winston from Regent University advocates placing people where their skills, abilities, and spiritual gifts best match the requirements of the position because this is where each person can best serve the organization (Winston B., 2002). According to Dr. John Kotter, many organizations have a leadership deficit because the organization ignores the leadership potential in the members of that organization, thereby, not offering training or relevant role models to raise up leaders from within (Kotter, 2005). Adopting a culture of continuous improvement throughout an organization, unleashes the stored resources of everyone involved in managing and implementing any change process. It also breeds individual ownership of the program, and a sense of fulfillment and contribution to the overall success.

A Common Core of Competencies for Innovative Leaders

Change and innovation work hand-in-hand. Few would argue against the notion that today's modern society is in the midst of a series of crises. However, that point of agreement is quickly lost in the search for solutions. One side claims to have the solutions while another side states that only they have the real answers. Confusion lies in the middle. Part of this confusion can be alleviated by identifying a common core of competencies for emerging innovative leaders. While much of the literature is focused on innovation, very little has been written about a common core of competencies. As an approach to organizational development, innovation leadership can be used to support the achievement of the mission or vision of an organization or group. In a world that is ever changing with new technologies and processes, it is becoming necessary for organizations to think innovatively in order to ensure their continued success and stay competitive. Emerging innovative leaders can begin the process of innovative leadership development by working on the following twelve common core competencies:

1. Core Values
2. Creativity
3. Strategic Mindset
4. Redesign
5. Trust
6. Ethics
7. Context
8. Forecasting
9. Rest & Renewal
10. Leadership Succession
11. Mentoring/Discipling
12. Understanding People

Essentially, the innovative leader must think and act as both an inspired, creative genius and the innovative general manager. According to research at Penn State University, innovative leaders must alternate among (Hunter, Steinberg, & Taylor, 2012):

- Facilitating broad, creative thinking about what is possible
- Bringing disparate ideas and consumer insights together into revolutionary product/service ideas
- Analyzing the business risk, financial return, and operational implications of taking the product to market
- Motivating a cross-functional team to collaborate
- Building support throughout the organization

Clearly, this role requires a resiliency to accept ambiguity and to toy with, reframe, and even abandon some ideas.

Without innovative leadership, organizations are more likely to struggle (McEntire & Greene-Shortridge, 2011). This new call for developing innovative leaders represents the shift from the 20th century, traditional view of organizational practices, which discouraged innovative behaviors, to the 21st century view of valuing innovative thinking as a potentially powerful influence on organizational performance (Mumford, Scott, Gaddis, & Strange, 2002).

Leadership is at the core of most successful ventures. However, what is at the core of the leader makes all the difference. Moral failures in leaders seem to be rampant in our modern society. Businesses are closing their doors in record numbers. The housing market is still in a crisis, and the value of the dollar has plummeted. Leaders are being pressed on all sides to produce answers and results. Effective cost and production ideas seem hard to come by today. What many people see as problems, innovative leaders see as opportunities.

Until now, the qualities of leadership that can successfully take a company into the future have been vague and ethereal. Success has been attributed to individuals with timing, or just at the right place, or with certain characteristics that only few "special" people will ever possess. It's time to solidify the once vague attributes and focus a plan on how to create leaders that are needed today and tomorrow. However, where do innovative leaders come from? What are the competencies or qualities of developing an innovative leader?

This book begins the dialogue of identifying distinguishing qualities or competencies to develop innovative leaders. The list is not comprehensive, but at least, identifies a starting point to begin the process for emerging leaders to develop in the quest to become an innovative leader. According to Rothwell, competency models are essential building blocks on which to begin a successful leadership framework (Rothwell, 2005, p. 83). Let's begin.

Chapter 1: Leadership: In the Beginning

"There is nothing more difficult to take in hand,
more perilous to conduct, or more uncertain in
its success, than to take the lead in the introduction
of a new order of things."
—Niccolo Machiavelli

"If your actions inspire others to dream more, learn more,
do more and become more, you are a leader."
—John Quincy Adams

Leadership existed in the mind of God long before the first thought of it came to man and is as old as time itself. In the Garden of Eden, the man, Adam, was created and instructed to provide leadership to all the earth in Genesis 1:26-31 (Spirit Filled Life Bible (NKJV), 1991):

> Then God said, "Let Us make man in Our image, according to Our likeness. They will rule the fish of the sea, the birds of the sky, the livestock, all the earth, and the creatures that crawl on the earth." So God created man in His own image; He created him in the image of God; He created them male and female. God blessed them, and God said to them, "Be fruitful, multiply, fill the earth, and subdue it. Rule the fish of the sea, the birds of the sky, and every creature that crawls on the earth. And God said, "See, I have given you every herb that yields seed which is on the face of all the earth, and every tree whose fruit yields seed; to you it shall be for food. Also, to every beast of the earth, to every bird of the air, and to

> everything that creeps on the earth, in which there is life, I have given every green herb for food"; and it was so. Then God saw everything that He had made, and indeed it was very good. So the evening and the morning were the sixth day."

The Lord God was the first teacher of leadership principles as He instructed Adam in taking care of the earth. It is important to note from Genesis 2:8 that the garden that was planted eastward in Eden came after the creation of Adam. The leadership mandate given by God Himself was to take care of the entire earth, not just a garden. This mandate was instituted before the creation of the garden as well as before the fall of mankind.

Five God-Developed Leadership Principles

Genesis 1:26-31 provides five observations that indicate God-developed leadership principles (Maxwell, 2002, p. 4):

- Being made in God's image means we were created to lead (v. 26).
- God commanded both male and female to have dominion. Leadership is not gender specific (v. 27).
- We are to rule over the earth, but not necessarily over each other. We were not directed to rule over each other, but over the earth's creatures (v. 28).
- All of us are to serve one another in the areas of our gifting and purpose. Our general purpose is to lead, but we each need to ask God about our specific purpose (v. 29, 30).
- All leadership is best exercised in the area of giftedness. When we discover our gifts, we will naturally lead where we are most productive, intuitive, comfortable, influential, and satisfied (v. 31).

Therefore, the journey to identify common core competencies of innovation leadership should start at the beginning. Since the Bible is generally considered one of the oldest books ever written, it provides an excellent starting point to begin the study of innovation leadership. However, proper study of any text requires an exegetical method of analysis. The Socio-Rhetorical Interpretation espoused by Vernon K. Robbins provides an outstanding tool for exegetical analysis because the focus is on the language itself. Malina may best describe the need for a social exegetical analysis method (Malina & Rohrbaugh, 1992, p. 2):

> It has become commonplace, of course, to recognize the time-and-place bounded-ness of the Bible. We know the New Testament to be the product of a small group of people living in the first century of the Common Era in the eastern Mediterranean region. But the distance between the world of that group and our own is usually calculated in historical terms, in terms of the flow of events or ideas that might account for what biblical texts ostensibly describe. Much scholarly effort has gone into telling that story. Such accounts are not sufficient, however, for understanding the position of the contemporary reader of the Bible. We must also recognize, as indeed recent social-scientific studies of the New Testament have begun to do, that the distance between ourselves and the Bible is social as well as temporal and conceptual. Such social distance includes radical differences in social structures, social roles, values, and general cultural features. In fact it may be that such social distance is the most fundamental distance of all. It may have had a greater impact on our ability to read and understand the Bible than most of what has preoccupied scholarly attention to date.

Rhetorical analysis is a method of close reading (criticism) that employs the principles of rhetoric to examine the interactions between a text, an author, and an audience. The focus is more on what the text "does" than what it "is". This type of analysis may be performed against any text or image. Therefore, it serves as a valuable tool for research and analysis in the hands of innovative leaders. Recognizing the need to identify with the social aspects of the Bible, Robbins identifies five different angles to explore multiple textures within texts in his Socio-Rhetorical Interpretation model (Robbins, 1996, pp. 3-4):

1. Inner Texture has features like the repetition of particular words, the creation of beginnings and endings, alternation of speech and

storytelling, particular ways in which the words present arguments, and the particular feel or aesthetic of the text. This focus is on the language itself and uses six types of inner texture analyses to discover patterns. The six types of inner texture analyses and patterns are the repetitive texture and pattern, progressive texture and pattern, narrational texture and pattern, argumentative texture and pattern, opening-middle-closing texture and pattern, and the sensory-aesthetic texture and pattern.

2. Intertexture concerns a text's configuration of phenomena that lie outside the text. A major goal of Intertextual analysis is to ascertain the nature and result of processes of configuration and reconfiguration of phenomena in the world outside the text from four patterns; the Oral-Scribal Intertexture, Cultural Intertexture, Social Intertexture, and Historical Intertexture.

3. Social and cultural texture—not to be confused with social and cultural inter-texture—concerns the capacities of the text to support social reform, withdrawal, or opposition and to evoke cultural perceptions of dominance, subordinance, difference, or exclusions. Specific social topics in the text exhibit resources for changing people or social practices, for destroying and re-creating social order, for withdrawing from present society to create one's own social world, or for coping with the world by transforming one's own perceptions of it.

4. Ideological texture begins with people, and defines ideology as an integrated system of beliefs, assumptions, and values. It is concerned with the alliance and conflicts within the language of the text as well as the way the text, and its interpreters, position themselves relative to other individuals and groups in that time. The individual locations sub-texture is the first step toward ideological texture analysis. It is characterized by the individuals' involved in the text responses to the world as well as the individuals' cultural location. Robbins uses the ideological texture to focus on the socio-cultural background and individual location

as well as the perspective of the writers and readers of the text. DeSilva identifies that ideological texture recognizes that a text is not just a vehicle for ideas but rather a vehicle by which the author hopes to achieve a certain goal (DeSilva, 2004, p. 25).

5. Sacred texture analysis describes a systemic and creative study of Scripture that provides insights regarding the nature of the relationship between divine life and human life. Robbins concludes that a sacred text features one or more people who have a special relationship to God, and the holy person par excellence in the New Testament is Jesus the Christ, which is regularly identified from New Testament texts as Christology. Shillington indicates that sacred texture refers to biblical text from a religious community to a religious community, and when complemented with theological interpretation yields valuable results (Shillington, 2002, p. 279). Cummings determines that creation may represent one of the first acts of the self-emptying service of God, and the self-emptying act of the Word becoming flesh another (Cummings, 2004).

Through the use of the Socio-Rhetorical Interpretation, proper exegetical analysis and exposition of the wisdom of God can be made accessible for innovative leaders. One layer of this wisdom can be uncovered through the use of socio-rhetorical analysis in the development of leadership ideologies as described in John chapter one.

From the beginning of the Old Testament through the New Testament, the development of leadership principles continued. When the wise men from the East came to King Herod and inquired about the birth of the King of the Jews, he consulted his chief priests and scribes. Using the intertexture analysis developed by Robbins on Matthew 2:5-6 the hidden truth of their reply is uncovered (HCSB, 2010, pp. 493-499):

> "In Bethlehem of Judea," they told him, "because this is what was written by the prophet: **And you, Bethlehem**, in the land of Judah, are by no means **least among the leaders of Judah: because out of you will come a leader who will shepherd My people Israel."**

These Scriptures are an example of the recitation analysis with replication of exact words [as highlighted in bold] with one or more differences of the Oral-Scribal Intertexture, which is when language is used from another text (Robbins, 1996, p. 40). This analysis can be used to reveal the leadership characteristic of Jesus as a leader or ruler that focuses on being a shepherd. The actual text referenced comes from Micah 5:2-5 (HCSB, 2010):

> Bethlehem Ephrathah, you are small among the clans of Judah; One will come from you to be ruler over Israel for Me. His origin is from antiquity, from eternity. Therefore, He will abandon them until the time when she who is in labor has given birth; then the rest of His brothers will return to the people of Israel. He will stand and shepherd them in the strength of Yahweh, in the majestic name of Yahweh His God. They will live securely, for then His greatness will extend to the ends of the earth. He will be their peace. When Assyria invades our land, when it marches against our fortresses, we will raise against it seven shepherds, even eight leaders of men.

One of the primary differences is that the chief priests and scribes that counseled Herod changed the prophecy from being a ruler in Micah 5:2 to being a shepherd. The Hebrew word *mashal* is used in Micah 5:2 and is properly translated "ruler" (Strong, 1981, Strong's Number 4910). Mashal is used 81 times in the Old Testament and is consistently translated ruler, governor, or master (Wigram, 1979, p. 774). This is consistent with the identification of Jesus as a servant-leader. Leadership development principles exist in extra-biblical materials as well.

4500 Year Old Leadership Principles Still Work

Outside of the Bible, the oldest and most complete literary work on leadership may be ***The Instruction of Ptah-Hotep***, which was written during the Fifth Egyptian Dynasty and dates from approximately 2495 to 2345 B.C. This papyrus relays the rules of behavior that all wise men should pass to their children and contains 50 maxims to live and govern by according to Ptah-Hotep, the Vizier of Egypt. These maxims included the following examples (Gunn, 2004):

1. Set a Good Example
2. Follow the Path of Truth
3. Be Kind and Receive Kindness in Return
4. Be Industrious, Fair to Your Neighbors and Pay Your Taxes
5. The Blessing of Children
6. Honor the Advancement of Others and Serve a Wise Man
7. Work Hard, Be Not Slothful
8. Take Time to Refresh Your Spirit
9. Love Your Neighbor and You will Prosper
10. Be Not Covetous with Your Neighbors
11. Cherish Your Wife
12. Guard Your Reputation

The Sun Tzu of Leadership

Sun Tzu may be considered the "Ptah-Hotep" of China. In approximately 500 B.C., the military leaders under the command of Sun Tzu put their collective wisdom into written form, and their 7000 word text was to shape the strategic thinking of all Asia in what is commonly called ***The Art of War.*** (The Denma Translation Group, 2003, p. 1). This text is still studied by military strategists and leaders around the world as well as at every military academy in the United States.

Former U.S. Chairman of the Joint Chiefs of Staff General Colin Powell said, "I've read the Chinese classic ***The Art of War*** written by Sun Tzu. He has been studied for hundreds of years and continues to give inspiration to soldiers and politicians. So every American soldier in the army knows of his works. We require our soldiers to read it (McNeilly, 1996, p. 73)." ***The Art of War*** is not just for military leaders. According to Michaelson, the lessons of Sun Tzu can be applied to real-life situations and serve as an everyday resource for all kinds of strategic thought especially strategic issues for business leaders and managers (Michaelson, 2001, pp. xx-xxi). Since the beginning of time, leadership principles have been used and passed down to other generations. Yet, efforts to identify a common core of competencies seem to be in its infancy for emerging innovative leaders.

Chapter 2
The Emerging Innovative Leader

"All men by nature desire knowledge."
—Aristotle

"We cannot solve problems by using the same kind of thinking we used when we created them."
—Albert Einstein

"I cannot help fearing that men may reach a point where they look on every new theory as a danger, every innovation as a toilsome trouble, every social advance as a first step toward revolution, and that they may absolutely refuse to move at all."
—Alexis de Tocqueville

The single most critical factor in the success or failure of an organization is leadership and that the leader's effectiveness is measured by the success of the organization (Bass B. , 2008, p. 11). The integrated definition of leadership provided by Winston and Patterson tie the leaders' ability to select, equip, train, and influence followers directly to a coordinated effort to achieve the organizational mission and objectives (Winston & Patterson, 2006):

> A leader is one or more people who selects, equips, trains, and influences one or more follower(s) who have diverse gifts, abilities, and skills and focuses the follower(s) to the organization's mission and objectives causing the follower(s) to willingly and enthusiastically expend spiritual, emotional, and

> physical energy in a concerted coordinated effort to achieve the organizational mission and objectives. The leader achieves this influence by humbly conveying a prophetic vision of the future in clear terms that resonates with the follower(s) beliefs and values in such a way that the follower(s) can understand and interpret the future into present-time action steps. In this process, the leader presents the prophetic vision in contrast to the present status of the organization and through the use of critical thinking skills, insight, intuition, and the use of both persuasive rhetoric and interpersonal communication including both active listening and positive discourse, facilitates and draws forth the opinions and beliefs of the followers such that the followers move through ambiguity toward clarity of understanding and shared insight that results in influencing the follower(s) to see and accept the future state of the organization as a desirable condition worth committing personal and corporate resources toward its achievement. The leader achieves this using ethical means and seeks the greater good of the follower(s) in the process of action steps such that the follower(s) is/are better off (including the personal development of the follower as well as emotional and physical healing of the follower) as a result of the interaction with the leader. The leader achieves this same state for his/her own self as a leader, as he/she seeks personal growth, renewal, regeneration, and increased stamina–mental, physical, emotional, and spiritual–through the leader-follower interactions.

According to Northouse, leadership occurs when others begin to recognize and look towards an individual in the group, regardless of the any title, as becoming the most influential member of the group or organization; this type of leadership occurs over time and is called emergent leadership (Northouse, 2007, p. 5). The development of the emergent innovative leader becomes vital to the continual success of the organization.

Diversity Strengthens Emerging Innovative Leader

One of the many challenges for innovative leadership development is to cultivate an emergent innovative leader that is able to transcend cultures and be effective in today's multi-cultural environment. According to Shahin and Wright, most leadership theories come from North America and may not be applicable across diverse cultures and ethnic groups which differ from the American culture (Shahin & Wright, 2004). As far back as 1993, researchers were highlighting that the current emphasis on management was primarily an American invention and that many other nations practice an entirely different form of management, which needs to be understood (Hofstede G., 1993). Additionally, research indicates that integrating cultural diversity change into leadership development can help companies better develop leaders' strengths to improve aspects of culture within a specific department or the overall company, which will further guarantee that leaders are fully focused on achieving organizational goals (Emerald Group Publishing, 2011). Cultural integration becomes a vital component to the development of emergent innovative leaders and needs to be integrated into the basic leadership theories.

Three Basic Theories

According to Bass, three basic theories can be used to explain how anyone can become leaders (Bass B. , 1990). Since these theories were designed to identify basic theories on leadership development, they would also apply to the developing of the emergent innovative leader. These theories are:

1. The Trait Theory: Certain personality traits may lead people naturally into leadership roles.
2. The Great Events Theory: A crisis or important event may cause a person to rise to the occasion and develop/exhibit extraordinary leadership qualities in an ordinary person.
3. The Transformational or Process Leadership Theory: Individuals choose to become leaders and, therefore, learn leadership skills.

The Trait Theory

The trait theory is also known as the Great-Man Theory. Colorful phrases such as "he was born to lead" and "she is a natural leader" are used to identify this theory. Bass reports that these theories draw attention to specific qualities of leaders and until the 1940's much of the research about leadership focused on these individual traits (Bass B., 2008, p. 49). Theorists identify many historical leaders under this heading; for example, without Moses, the children of Israel would have remained in Egypt and without Winston Churchill, the British would have surrendered in 1940 (Bass B., 2008, p. 48).

The Great Event Theory

The great events theory is also known as situational theories, which is dependent upon the concept that leadership is a matter of situational demands, and these situational factors will determine who emerges as a leader; this theory is in direct opposition to the traits theory and is particularly favored in the Unites States (Bass B., 2008, p. 52). Other research also calls this theory the momentous event theory which introduces personal uncertainty into the relational structure of the leader and describes momentous events as distinctive, circumscribed, and highly emotional (Olivares, 2011). Pillemer defines momentous events as follows (Pillemer, 2011):

- The memory represents a specific event that took place at a particular time and place.
- It contains a detailed account of the person's own personal circumstances at the time; the memory includes sensory imagery (visual, auditory, olfactory, or tactile).
- The "rememberer" believes that the event actually happened.

1 Samuel 17 describes a momentous event when a young boy named David rose to the situation that was challenging the nation of Israel under King Saul. This momentous event and David's victory over Goliath eventually leads David to become the next king of Israel. President George W. Bush

responds to the momentous event of the terrorist attacks on 911, and no other attack occurs during his presidency.

The Transformational Theory

The transformational or process leadership theory is among the new theories of leadership development. For the empirical study of leadership, transformational leadership was a new paradigm or a change of views that was first formalized as a theory by James Burns in 1978 (Bass B., 2008, p. 50). According to Burns, the transforming leader looks for potential motives in followers, seeks to satisfy higher needs, and engages the full person of the follower to result in a mutual relationship that converts followers into leaders (Burns, 1978, p. 4). Bass also defines transformational leadership in terms of how the leader affects followers, who are intended to trust, admire and respect the transformational leader when he identified three ways in which leaders transform followers (Bass B., 2008, p. 50):

- Increasing their awareness of task importance and value
- Getting them to focus first on team or organizational goals, rather than their own interests
- Activating their higher-order needs

Transformational Leadership

Burns defines a transformational leader as one who raises the followers' level of consciousness about the importance and value of outcomes and how to effectively reach them (Burns, 1978). The obvious emphasis is upon the followers. Bass concludes that transformational leadership is about changing people and transformational leaders motivate their followers to do more than they originally intended or thought possible (Bass B., 2008).

Many transformational leaders are also charismatic in nature. Khurana issues a caution concerning charismatic-only leaders when he states that the charismatic succession process implies that a single individual deserves vastly more attention and rewards than anyone else in the organization, and ignores the reality that organizational performance is driven by more than one person (Khurana, 2002, p. 197). Bass relates the dynamics of the charismatic leader-follower relationship and concludes that charismatic leaders often use themselves as examples for their subordinates to follow (Bass B., 2008, p. 590). Northouse identifies four specific types of charismatic behavior (Northouse, 2007, pp. 178-179):

- They are strong role models for the beliefs and values they want their followers to adopt.
- They appear competent to followers.
- They articulate ideological goals that have moral overtones.
- They communicate high expectations for followers and they exhibit confidence in their followers' abilities to meet these expectations.

The study of transformational and charismatic leadership is relatively recent, but the research has been steadily growing. Burns first introduced the transforming leader in 1978 when he concluded that transforming leadership was best built upon a relationship of mutual stimulation and elevation that converts followers into leaders and leaders into moral agents (Burns, 1978). While charismatic leadership can be regarded as part of transformational leadership, some research indicates that the undesirable consequences at the societal level of charismatic leadership include totalitarian aspects as well as truth manipulation practiced by some charismatic leaders (Aaltio-Marjosola & Takala, 2000).

Servant Leadership

It is also important to distinguish servant leadership from transformation leadership. According to Stone, Russell and Patterson, transformational leaders direct their focus toward the organization, so their behavior builds follower commitment toward organizational objectives, while servant leaders focus on their followers, and the achievement of organizational objectives is a subordinate outcome (Stone, Russell, & Patterson, 2004). Kotter concludes that many organizations have a leadership deficit because the organization ignores the leadership potential in the members of that organization, thereby, not offering training or relevant role models to raise up leaders from within (Kotter, 2005). Deming outlines three steps to get others involved in accomplishing transformative change (Deming, 1994):

- The transformative leader has a theory and understands why the transformation would bring gains to the organization as well as the people involved in the organization.
- The transformative leader feels compelled to accomplish the transformation as an obligation to the people and the organization.
- The transformative leader has a step-by-step plan and can explain it in simple terms.

A transformational leader can make the organization more successful by valuing its human capital. Northouse determined that the effect of organizational change through transformational leaders is the ability of the transformational leader to be a role model, create a vision and empower followers to facilitate ownership of the process (Northouse, 2007). However, transformational leadership is not just a Christian church or North American concept. From a cross-cultural perspective, Dr. Y.L.J. Lam from the Chinese University of Hong Kong concludes that transformational leadership is a very effective type of leadership in many cultural settings (Lam, 2002). Bass identifies that charismatics can foster antisocial behavior, and personalized charismatic leaders can be dominant, self-interested, and authoritarian (Bass B., 2008, p. 578). While charismatic and transformational leadership styles are similar, there are some differences; especially when measured against the servant leadership style.

Transformational leadership is considered by many to be closest to the "prototype" of leadership that people have in mind when they describe an ideal leader which is more likely to provide a role model with which followers want to identify as well as emulate (Bass B., 2008, p. 51). However, the "ideal" type of leader can be found in John chapter one, and analyzed through Robbins' Socio-Rhetorical Interpretation.

Inner Texture

As previously stated, the inner texture method of exegetical analysis studies the contextual placement of words to enhance the overall meaning and understanding of a text. According to Robbins, this approach centers on values, convictions and beliefs of a text (Robbins, 1996, p. 1). It focuses on certain features in the language used such as repeated words and how the words look and feel. Again, the focus is on the language itself.

Repetitive Texture and Pattern

According to Robbins, the repetitive texture and pattern analysis focuses on the words and phrases that occur more than once in the selected text (Robbins, 1996, p. 8). This repetitive occurrence provides an initial glimpse into the rhetorical movements of the text. This data from John 1:1-17 (NKJV) is best represented in Table 1 from John 1:

The analysis of the data from table 1 indicates that the Apostle John was creating a connection to the Book of Genesis to take the reader back to the days before creation to introduce Jesus. Not only are the first three words of both books the same but he also emphasizes that God and the Word worked together and made all things. In Genesis 1:28 God said, "let Us make man in Our image according to Our likeness" (NKJV). Continuing the connection to Genesis, John emphasizes that the light was not only the light of men but also dispelled darkness. Of course, the first act of creation in Genesis was the creation of light. The creation theme in Genesis concludes with the creation of man and John notes the importance of God's use and creation of mankind.

Emerging innovative leaders can ascertain from the repetitive texture of John 1:1-17 the need to emphasize an organization's connection to their people and to the organization's foundation. History and heritage can be used to bring successive generations together in order to keep an organization moving forward. Innovative leaders should work to develop their followers and tie them to the success of the group. Grace and truth becomes the substance that keeps the company on the right track. Bass calls this the identification process in his characteristics of leaders as leaders and followers begin to identify with one another to produce a collective identity (Bass B., 2008, p. 589).

Progressive Texture and Pattern

Developing out of the repetitive texture, the progressive texture and pattern looks at the sequence of the words and phrases (Robbins, 1996, p. 10). John is clearly following a progressive pattern as he connects his writings to the Old Covenant and then progresses to the transition from the Law in the

1	Beginning	Word Word Word	God God					
2	Beginning		God He					
3			Him Him	made made made				
4			Him			light		
5						light		
6			God					John man
7						light		man
8						light light		he
9						light light	world	man
10			He Him Him	made			world world world	
11			He His His Him					own own
12			Him He His name					them children of God
13			God					Man
14		Word	His Father		grace and truth			us we
15			Him He He He					John I me me me
16			His		grace grace			we
17			Jesus		grace and truth			
Totals	2	4	28	4	4	7	4	17

Table 1 of Repetitive Texture for John 1:1-17 (NKJV)

Old Covenant to the New Covenant in Jesus Christ. Using many of the same words and sequence of words from the book of Genesis, John shows the progression from the Old Covenant teaching of the Law to the New Covenant teaching of Jesus Christ. John further works to tie his writings to a much broader scope through the use of the Greek word *kosmos* which becomes translated "world" in the New King James Version.

Kosmos means an orderly arrangement to the world (Strong, 1981, p. 43). *Kosmos* ties very closely to the ordered days of creation in Genesis 1:1-31. John uses *kosmos* over 75 times just in his Gospel as well as another 25 times in his letters of I, II, and III John (Wigram, 1979, pp. 429-430). John is clearly developing a progressive theme in the continual use of kosmos to refer to the order of things and not to the geophysical or biological world (Hayford, 1995, p. 314). John progresses before creation to his present day and emphasizes that Jesus has been there all along. Contemporary organizations can learn the need to develop a unique business culture that continues throughout time to develop its leaders and followers.

The Walt Disney Company would be an example of this principle. When Walt Disney was alive he was completely engaged in creating the Disney culture. However, Walt Disney suddenly dies and the company has to decide who was going to continue the culture of creation. After weeks of deliberation, the Disney Company decided that Walt Disney was still going to be used to create the culture. All the executives who worked personally with Walt Disney gathered together and began to write down all the things that they could remember that Walt would do and say. From this workshop, the Traditions Course was developed and every cast member of the Disney organization is required to attend this course including the current Chief Executive Officer (Disney Institute, 2001, pp. 11-13). Since Walt Disney created the Disney culture, he would be the one to continue producing this culture long after he was gone.

Argumentative Texture and Pattern

The argumentative texture and pattern scans for any types of inner reasoning in the text (Robbins, 1996, p. 21). This line of reasoning can be logical or qualitative and is used to persuade the reader's thinking and actions. This text displays a qualitative and a logical pattern. The qualitative pattern looks at the quality of the images and descriptions to convince the reader to accept the portrayal of Jesus as the Christ. In this text, John uses citations and comparisons to the book of Genesis in order to persuade his readers that Jesus existed prior to any creation. From the logical perspective, if Jesus pre-dates the Law, the logical conclusion would be to follow Him instead of the Law. John begins his argumentative texture starting in verse one. In verse six, John produces a witness in the form of John the Baptist to verify and validate the claims about Jesus. John continues in verses 14-17 that Jesus existed not only before creation but actually became flesh and walked among people.

Emerging innovative leaders can learn about the need to be persuasive and motivational to their followers from this analysis. As organizations grow, new leaders are constantly stepping up to positions of authority. These leaders can come from within the organization as long as the organization is taking the time to develop, train and mentor these new leaders. Since the goal of this texture is persuasion and motivation, organizations that promote from within will demonstrate that focused work for the group good will be rewarded. Many times, other organizations will persuade some of the best talent to leave one company for another. One of the best arguments to stay with a company is the knowledge that the company has your best interests in mind when you have the company's best interests in mind. Promotion can come from internally instead of moving around from company to company. Just as John wants to persuade his readers to stay with Jesus, organizations need to be able to persuade their best talent to stay. Bass states that leaders should work to include the worth of the individual to produce a collective history and a productive future (Bass B., 2008, p. 589).

Narrational Texture and Pattern

Narrational texture reflects the voice or voices through which the words of the text speak (Robbins, 1996, p. 15). This pattern moves the discourse forward. The use of the narrational pattern in this text reveals that John is the one speaking and he is guiding the readers through a series of past events to set things in order. The focus of this narrative is to move the readers from the time before creation and establish that Jesus was already there through the current time to establish that Jesus is still here. John is using the narrational commentary to accomplish more than simply relating a story. He is setting the stage that Jesus existed before anything else, and that He has made available to everyone the fullness of God in a personal relationship with the Father. John sets the stage that Jesus is the Word made flesh and walked among His people. He continues this narrational theme throughout much of the gospel building upon its key verse in John 3:16 that God so loved the kosmos that He gave His only Son to get things set back in order.

Emerging innovative leaders can learn from the narrational portion of this text that it is important to set the stage in broader terms than just the daily routine of work. Whether the company is a business or a ministry, day-in day-out work can become mundane and trivial. However, as the company sets the stage for how that work is being used to promote a greater good and to support a greater cause, the followers and the leaders can begin to see the bigger picture. Bass explains that eloquence and rhetoric are vital to the development of a leaders' team (Bass B., 2008, p. 586). Miller concludes that every leader leads through the process of team building (Miller, 1995, p. 166)

Opening-Middle-Closing Texture and Pattern

The uniqueness of this pattern is that it divides the text into three parts for analysis; the beginning, the body and the conclusion (Robbins, 1996, p. 19). John follows this pattern by starting at the beginning of creation to show Jesus was already there. He continues at the body part of the analysis by stating that Jesus became flesh. The conclusion analysis demonstrates that the fullness of God is available through Jesus who moves past the law and into grace and truth. The leadership principle for innovative leaders would be that leaders and followers need a structure or plan identifying where the company has been and where it is going. According to Miller, all leaders need a structure for their vision or it will lose its definition and purpose (Miller, 1995, p. 98).

Sensory-Aesthetic Texture and Pattern

The sensory-aesthetic pattern is associated with the senses of thought, emotion, sight, sound, touch, and smell along with their interaction (Robbins, 1996, pp. 29-30). Typically, these patterns can be described as three types of zones; the zone of self-expressive speech, the zone of emotion-fused thought, and the zone of purposeful action. John engages all three of these zones. Self-expressive speech starts the gospel in John 1:1 with the choice of the words from Genesis 1:1 "in the beginning" expressing that Jesus existed before the creation of the earth. As an emotion-fused thought, John uses verses 10-12 to claim that the world that He had created did not know Him or receive Him; yet, He received them. John demonstrates purposeful action in John 1:14 and introduces the incarnate savior in the form of Jesus Christ when the Word became flesh and dwelt among His people.

Emerging innovative leaders can implement this in the roles of leaders and followers as they use verbal and nonverbal cues to interact together. Leaders and followers need to be able to articulate their feelings and emotions to one another to learn interdependence. Bass identifies these types of patterns as expressive behavior and insight (Bass B., 2008, pp. 584-585).

The Apostle John surveyed the needs of his day and the present condition of the church to present his gospel message. John starts from the beginning that Jesus existed before the beginning to establish that only Jesus is the way the truth and the life. The exegetical method of Socio-Rhetorical Criticism's inner texture analysis of John 1:1-17 begins to reveal the depth of the message that John wanted to convey in his gospel. The use of this method is not only productive for exegetical analysis placing the text in time and place, but it also can be used to uncover leadership /followership principles for emerging innovative leaders. This type of analysis provides the foundation for the common core competencies.

Chapter 3
The Common Core of Core Values

"Your beliefs become your thoughts. Your thoughts become your words. Your words become your actions. Your actions become your habits. Your habits become your values. Your values become your destiny."
—Mahatma Gandhi

"At all costs we must re-establish faith in spiritual values. We must worship something beyond ourselves, lest we destroy ourselves."
—Sir Philip Gibbs (1877-1962)
English Journalist and Novelist

Core values are required for innovative leaders to begin building a common core of competencies. The foundation of core values should come from an unchangeable source that has survived the test of time over the years. The only source that has been proven accurate over and over again is the Bible, which is the Word of God. However, for some people and organizations, the Bible seems to be outdated and out of touch with today's modern society. Yet, core values have to be rooted in something. Values that have their root in subjectivity and relativism such as secular humanism begin to cause skepticism as well as uncertainty. The uncertainty of core values rooted in relativism produces a foundation that cannot be stable as it shifts in the current subjectivity of the moment. This type of uncertain foundation produces a shaky organization with little substance or long term future. The core values of people and organizations become the lens through which they view the world.

Many organizations today look at institutional values from a core values perspective, which is similar to the core strategy component described by Hamel. According to Hamel, core strategy is one of four major components of a business model and is closely related to the business mission, which captures the overall objective and purpose of the organization (Hamel, 2000, p. 70). From this core strategy, organizations derive their core values. Cameron and Quinn identify that core values, along with assumptions, interpretations, and approaches that characterize organizations, are defined according to the culture of the organization (Cameron & Quinn, 2011, p. 35). Organizational culture comes from the beliefs of the individuals inside the organization. McKinney notes that an effective leader has an agenda designed to produce results, but must be guided by a core set of values (McKinney, 2011). Loo concludes that core values are the fundamental beliefs, morals, and standards that define and guide a person's behavior; while other aspects of life change, core values do not change (Loo, 2006).

Believers and followers of Jesus Christ need to consider how their commitment to Him affects not only their political and ethical convictions, but also the way they think and act about theology, philosophy, ethics, biology, psychology, sociology, law, politics, economics, and history. This collection of convictions is called a worldview (Noebel, 2006, p. 205). In the marketplace of core values, worldviews provide the source for these values and are in competition for the ideologies of today's leaders. Noebel identifies two commonly conflicting worldviews: Biblical Christian and Secular Humanist (Noebel, 2006, pp. 209-210). According to Noebel, the current conflict of worldviews engulfing Western culture is designed to dethrone Jesus Christ and replace the Biblical Christian worldview with the ideas of fallible, but very clever human beings (Noebel, 2006, pp. 251-2).

The Biblical Christian Worldview

The Biblical Christian worldview should be based on the Bible and constructed around the person of Jesus Christ. This worldview focuses upon 2 Corinthians 10:5 by casting down arguments and every high thing that exalts itself against the knowledge of God, bringing every thought into captivity to the obedience of Christ. Biblical Christian ethics is inseparable from theology because it is grounded in the character of God. The task of Christian ethics, then, is to determine what conforms to God's character and what does not. Francis Schaeffer explains the uniqueness of the Biblical Christian worldview (Schaeffer, 1982):

> One of the distinctions of the Judeo-Christian God is that not all things are the same to Him. That at first may sound rather trivial, but in reality it is one of the most profound things one can say about the Judeo–Christian God. He exists; He has a character; and not all things are the same to Him. Some things conform to His character, and some are opposed to His character.

From the Biblical Christian worldview, values have to come from an unchanging, authoritative source which is the Word of God. C. S. Lewis says that Christians "are tempted to make unnecessary concessions to those outside the Faith. We give in too much. We must show our Christian colors, if we are to be true to Jesus Christ. We cannot remain silent and concede everything away (Lewis, God in the Dock, 2002, p. 62)."

Successful leaders must find a way to infuse and instill biblical values across the organization. Values can be used to unify and get people to work together. Jesus said in Matthew 12:25 that "every kingdom divided against itself is headed for destruction, and no city or house divided against itself will stand (Spirit Filled Life Bible (NKJV), 1991)." Organizations that do not have common Biblical values are walking down the path of failure. According to Winston, values have to be based on something (Winston B. , 2002, p. 1). One of the challenges that leaders face today is not knowing what they believe about the source of their beliefs and values. Pat Robertson concludes that the modern world is in a crisis in large part due to the unconstrained moral degradation of its leaders (Gyertson, 1993, p. 15). When morals and core values do not have a true north setting firmly grounded in the Bible, then the organization will drift off course and a new leader needs to rise up with biblical standards and morals to keep the organization on course. Gangel identifies that there is a growing encroachment of secular leaders bringing their secular styles of leadership into the church and add a Scripture verse to it in order to call it Christian

(Gangel, 1981, p. 19). As Christian leaders, it is vital to identify the source of our values as well as the worldview of those values before infusing and instilling them into our organizations.

Secular Humanism Worldview

Since the first Humanist Manifesto, secular humanist thinkers have sought to replace Christian moral values with ideas that enhance human development and social progress. Noebel determines that the ideas and philosophies of men and women such as Marx, Freud, Darwin, Nietzsche, Lenin, Stalin, Russell, Heidegger, Adorno, Lukacs, Gramsci, Sanger, Dewey, Kinsey, Sagan, Derrida, Foucault and others have led to an array of practices and lifestyles contrary to biblical values (Noebel, 2006, pp. 332-333). From the humanist point of view, self becomes the source of values. Joas suggests that the genesis of values originate in experiences of self-formation and self-transcendence (Joas, 2000, p. 145). Closely affiliated with the tenets of humanism is pragmatism, which is based upon self-experiential learning.

The basic framework of pragmatism, as espoused by John Dewey, contends that values must start with organic behavior, which places the foundation of values inside the human self (Joas, 2000, p. 106). Dewey sees the genesis of values as the creative work of people's imagination. Dewey was not only a pragmatist, but also a signatory on the first Humanist Manifesto in 1933, which states that humanism is a philosophical, religious, and moral point of view (Noebel, 2006, pp. 1150-1151). To the humanist, truth becomes an abstraction that is based upon relativism.

A leading secular humanist and postmodernist, Richard Rorty, concludes that truth cannot be out there—cannot exist independently of the human mind (Rorty, 1989, p. 53). Rorty further contends that truth and moral choice is a compromise between competing goods rather than a choice between absolute right and wrong (Rorty, 1999, p. 36). However, the Apostle Paul writes in I Timothy 3:15 that the pillar and foundation of truth is only found in God's Word, and, therefore, not in men. Noebel further explains that Nietzsche, Rorty, Dewey, and their followers say that there is no eternal Father, that faith in God is a mark of weakness or insanity, and that people and cultures create their own reality and morality (Noebel, 2006, pp. 277-278).

According to Packer and Howard, humanism has its appeal because it allows for the behavior that religion forbids, and the 1933 Manifesto presents a science-oriented ethic as an alternative religion which the US Supreme Court recognized as such in 1961 (Gyertson, 1993, p. 65). Gyertson reports that secular humanism is neither a professional field nor a character quality, but an aggressive cultural ideology that becomes a set of ideas expressed in programs designed to change people's lives (Gyertson, 1993, p. 61). Noebel states that relativism consists of little more than experimenting with ethics in every new scenario and when leaders choose to ignore all outside authority and all rational restrictions, boundless moral relativism results (Noebel, 2006). Packer and Howard also identify that the Humanist Manifesto I and II (1933 and 1973 respectively) state that "humanism sets human beings at the center of the universe maintaining that the nature of man is the most highly developed component to all that exists; that happiness and enrichment of human life now is all that should be considered; that scientific reason is the only tool needed for the task; and that Christianity hinders the enterprise rather than helps it (Gyertson, 1993, p. 64)."

As people and society turn away from the absolute standards of God's Word and begin to embrace the subjective standards of relativism and self, the actual moral fiber and standards of society begin to shift, disintegrate and decay. A current example of the conflict between the core values of the Biblical Christian worldview and the core values of the Secular Humanist worldview is the recent situation regarding comments made by the current president and Chief Operating Officer of Chick-fil-A, Dan Cathy, which is a Christian-owned family business with a long heritage of emphasizing the Biblical Christian worldview.

Chick-fil-A: The Definition of Marriage

According to the New York Times, this uproar began when Dan T. Cathy, whose deeply religious father, S. Truett Cathy started the company in 1967, told a Christian news organization that Chick-fil-A supported the biblical definition of the family unit (Severson, 2012). What the New York Times fails to mention is that Mr. Cathy's comments was in agreement with the federal government definition of marriage at that time. The 1996 Defense of Marriage Act of the 104th Congress established the federal definition of: (1) "marriage" as only a legal union between one man and one woman as husband and wife; and (2) "spouse" as only a person of the opposite sex who is a husband or wife (U.S. Congress, 1996). This Act was signed into law by then-President Bill Clinton. However, in 2013 section three of the Act was ruled as unconstitutional by the U.S. Supreme Court in *United States v. Windsor,* and the definition standard that has existed for many years starts to decay.

Character and values have always been at the forefront of Chick-fil-A, so the original statement came as no surprise. In a 2010 interview with Dan Cathy by *T+D Magazine*, which is a monthly business magazine published by The American Society for Training & Development, Mr. Cathy presented the Chick-fil-A formula for success (Bingham & Galagan, 2010):

> We look for what we call "the three Cs": competence, character, and chemistry. Competence is business acumen and the knowledge and skills to do the job. The job of the restaurant operator is evolving and growing. It used to be fairly simple. You'd have 15 people in a mall location that was 800 square feet doing $700,000 or $800,000 a year. Now, you're talking about 70 or 80 people in a 5,000-square-foot building doing $3 to $6 million in sales. We have four restaurants this year that may reach $6 million. It's a vastly different arena today, and we've had to adjust our expectations and the qualifications on competency. Character and values are hugely important to us because there can be brilliant people with MBAs and so on, but as several celebrities have shown us recently, you can have some skeletons in the closet. The financial consequences of those kinds of things are horrific. Moral choices and decisions do matter. They do count. When it comes to chemistry, we're looking for the ability to inspire, excite, and motivate other people. They say it's easier to get a job with the CIA than with us.

According to Truett Cathy, the founder of Chick-fil-A, next to a person's salvation the most important decision is choosing a spouse and marriage is a lifetime commitment to be taken seriously because it can make you or break you (Cathy, 1989, p. 81). Truett Cathy also tells the story of his son, Dan, when he was given his first automobile (Cathy, 1989, p. 97):

> I had a nameplate made that I had fastened to the dashboard. When I presented the car and handed Dan the keys, he walked around it, admiring it with great pride. He opened the door and immediately saw the nameplate of the dash. It read: Custom made for Dan Cathy—Matthew 6:33. "What's Matthew 6:33, Dad?" Dan asked. "Get your Bible and see." Dan ran into the house and looked up the verse: "But seek ye first the kingdom of God, and His righteousness; and all these things shall be added unto you" (KJV). I wanted Dan to receive the message that God had many blessings in store for him, materially and spiritually, if he would remember to seek God's guidance in every decision he made.

With this foundation in a Biblical Christian worldview, it is no wonder that Dan Cathy's core values for Chick-fil-A are biblically based. Dan Cathy also believes strongly that Christians are missionaries in the workplace. In a current interview with the *Baptist Press*, Cathy stated (Blume, 2012):

> "Jesus had a lot of things to say about people who work and live in the business community," he said. His goal in the workplace is "to take biblical truth and put skin on it...We're talking about how our performance in the workplace should be the focus of how we build respect, rapport and relationships with others that opens the gateway to interest people in knowing God. All throughout the New Testament there is an evangelism strategy related to our performance in the workplace...Our work should be an act of worship. Our work should be our mission field. As long as we are stateside, let's don't think we have to go on mission trips

> by getting a passport...If you're obedient to God you are going to be evangelistic in the quality of the work you do, using that as a portal to share [Christ]."

Chick-fil-A is a private family owned business with over 1600 restaurants and over 4 billion dollars in sales in 2012 (Blume, 2012). When asked if Chick-fil-A's success is attributed to biblical values, Cathy quickly said, "I think they're inseparable. God wants to give us wisdom to make good decisions and choices." Quoting James 1:5, he spoke of how often he asks God for wisdom. While Dan Cathy and Chick-fil-A's Biblical Christian Worldview and core values may be in conflict with the Secular Humanist worldviews and core values, sales are sky-rocketing and restaurant expansions are continuing to grow. From an organizational point of view, the source of their values and ethics are without question. Vital to the success of Chick-fil-A is their ability to clearly articulate their worldview and the source of their core values.

Building Core Values and Ethics

According to Daft, the source of values and ethics in an organization is both an individual and an organizational matter, and the standards for socially responsible conduct are embodied within each employee as well as the organization itself (Daft, 2007, p. 378). A core value becomes an absolute standard for a leader. An absolute standard has to come from a source that does not change over time. Only one source meets that criterion. Only the Bible and biblical principles have survived the test of time and scrutiny to become the only infallible and authoritative source from which true core values can be derived. The Word of God is the one true and trusted source that can be used in the development of an absolute standard. Perhaps George Washington best described this need in his first inaugural address as the President of the United States when he said, "We ought to be no less persuaded that the propitious smiles of Heaven can never be expected on a nation that disregards the eternal rules of order and right which Heaven itself has ordained (Washington, 1789)."

General Norman Schwarzkopf said that "Leadership involves conduct. Conduct is determined by values. Values are what make us who we are

(Schwarzkopf, 1992, p. 274)." The journey of a leader or organization through self-evaluation becomes a building process which starts with core values and worldviews. Kouzes and Posner claim that core values are directly relevant to credibility and enable people to know in their own minds what to do and not do (Kouzes & Posner, 1993, p. 61). Thomas and Susan Kuczmarski conclude that people need values that they can believe in but, due to mergers and downsizing of the last decade, age old norms of employment security have gone by the wayside, and as a result many American organizations have lost the spirit and loyalty of their workforce as well as their competitive edge (Kuczmarski & Kuczmarski, 1995, p. 6). The self-evaluation of values is also strongly influenced by a person's background and culture. Research at the University of the South Pacific in Fiji identified that culture influences our thinking and consequently our behaviors, and social justice is about recognizing our values, philosophies, processes, and structures in our education system and that theorizing social justice should be founded on our knowledge systems that are embedded in our cultures (Fua, 2007).

Dolan and Richley conclude that the philosophy of management by core values will produce a more successful organization than management by instruction or management by objectives and that the philosophy of management by values has been successful (Dolan & Richley, 2006). Christian leaders today need to be more like the sons of Issachar in I Chronicles 12:32 where the sons of Issachar had an understanding of the times to know what Israel ought to do.

Organizations need a fresh norms-and-values infusion because values-less leadership, as well as a lack of commitment to values, are two primary factors that decrease employee satisfaction and production (Kuczmarski & Kuczmarski, 1995, p. 58). Looking towards the inner being as the source of values will never produce good results. Jesus said in Matthew 15:19 that from the heart come evil thoughts, murders, adulteries, sexual immoralities, thefts, and false testimonies. C. S. Lewis notes that we are now getting to the point at which different beliefs about the universe lead to different behavior and religion involves a series of statements about facts, which must be either true or false; if they are true, one set of conclusions will follow about the right sailing of the human fleet, if they are false, quite another set (Lewis, 1972, p. 58). Chick-fil-A attributes their success to their Biblical Christian worldview as their source of values. Successful leaders today need to able to clearly articulate their worldview and source of core values. Secular humanists would benefit from reading and understanding the Apostle Paul in 1 Corinthians 1:20, "Where is the philosopher? Where is the scholar? Where is the debater of this age? Hasn't God made the world's wisdom foolish? (Spirit Filled Life Bible (NKJV), 1991)" Innovative leaders from the Biblical Christian worldview with a biblical source of core values would say, yes and amen.

Chapter 4
The Common Core of Creativity

"In the Beginning, God CREATED."
—Genesis 1:1

"Everybody born comes from the Creator trailing wisps of glory. We come from the Creator with creativity. I think that each one of us is born with creativity."
—Maya Angelou

"A discovery is said to be an accident meeting a prepared mind."
—Albert Szent-Gyorgyi

Creativity and innovation originated with God when He spoke the world into existence and breathed life into man. While mankind will never be able to top that, mankind would be wise to start with the presence of God for creativity and innovation. Robbins identifies that God's presence provides a starting point for analyzing as well as interpreting the sacred texture of a text, which he calls the deity portion of a text (Robbins, 1996, p. 120). Like the Inner Texture analysis used in chapter two, using the Sacred Texture analysis on John chapter one also indicates that the Apostle John was creating a connection to the Book of Genesis to take the reader back to the days before creation to introduce Jesus. Again, the first three words of both books are the same and John emphasizes that God and the Word worked together and made all things.

The First Goal of Creativity

Robbins concludes that the sacred texture analysis describes a systemic and creative study of scripture that provides insights regarding the nature of the relationship between divine life and human life (Robbins, 1996, p. 120). Shillington indicates that sacred texture refers to biblical text from a religious community to a religious community, and when complemented with theological interpretation yields valuable results (Shillington, 2002, p. 279). Cummings determines that creation may represent one of the first acts of the self-emptying service of God, and the self-emptying act of the Word becoming flesh another (Cummings, 2004). Both creation and incarnation reveal God's presence and action in divine history. The sacred texture analysis of John chapter one reveals how historical events such as creation and the incarnation represent purposeful steps in the coming of the kingdom of God, and God's actions behind the scenes of history with a plan established by God. Therefore, the first goal for creativity and innovation should be to tap into that unlimited resource.

Michalko concludes that creativity is decided by what people choose to do and what they refuse to do (Michalko, 2006, p. xv). To release creativity requires seeing something different than everyone else. Albert Szent-Györgyi, a Hungarian-born biochemist who won the Nobel Prize in 1937, stated that creativity and discovery consist of seeing what everybody has seen and thinking what nobody has thought (Szent-Gyorgyi, 1962). According to Oster, creativity requires a careful tending process and everyone must be absolutely sure that wild and unusual ideas are welcomed as well as ensuring that any impediments to creativity are removed (Oster, 2011, pp. 18-19).

The Greatest Challenge to Creativity

Perhaps the greatest challenge to releasing creativity is the stifling of the creative process that is required to think innovatively. Businesses where creativity is not valued and nurtured will struggle to compete with more visionary enterprises because innovative leadership requires creativity in order to produce effective results (Strategic Direction, 2008). Cooper contends that creativity plays a vital role in the innovative thinking process in order to produce a sustained competitive advantage but also admits that many organizations actually discourage the freedom of practicing creativity (Cooper, 1998). Oster concludes that creative thinkers and innovators never seem to be corporate insiders much less those on the organizational fast track and many times they need organizational cover from corporate fire since they do everything possible to escape the shackles of precedent, tradition, and orthodoxy (Oster, 2011, pp. 236-237). According to Gryskiewicz, creativity and innovation have been found to be the cornerstone of healthy organizations that are ready for reinventing themselves, and organizations accomplish this by being relevant to changing markets as well as the use of new technology (Gryskiewicz, 1999, p. 1).

When Einstein was asked to identify the difference between himself and an average person, he responded that an average person looking for a needle in a haystack would stop looking after finding the needle, but he (Einstein) would continue to look through the entire haystack to find all the needles (Michalko, 2001, p. 3). Today's leaders can create environments that facilitate and encourage employee creativity by empowering collaboration through the sharing of tacit knowledge. Oguz and Sengün contend that tacit knowledge as a concept has its origins in Michael Polanyi's writings whose aim was to bring forward the inarticulate dimension of human knowing (Oguz & Sengün, 2011). Tacit knowledge can be a source of a huge range of opportunities and potentials that constitute discovery and creativity as employees must be given the time, space and opportunity to transfer and, therefore, share tacit knowledge which is transmitted verbally (Seidler-de Alwis & Evi, 2008). This sharing becomes a key enabler of collaboration. According to Stagich, leaders in the new millennium must understand how to work successfully in collaborations across nationalities and cultures (Stagich, 2006, Kindle Locations 89-92).

Zweifel determines that global leaders, managers, and entrepreneurs must also become global citizens that will know what gifts to bring to dinner in Singapore as well as how to run a consensus-building meeting in Germany (Zweifel, 2003, p. 75). Von Krough et al. conclude that tacit knowledge is the most important source of creativity, yet it is often underutilized in an organization and difficult to separate from productive work (Von Krogh, Ichijo, & Nonaka, 2000, p. 176). Branson from the Australian Catholic University affirms the need to develop a more human organization that meets the needs of the people in the organization by paying attention to their sense of self and organizational leaders need to restore the meaning of work by involving workers collaboratively in decisions that affect them personally and professionally (Branson, 2009, p. 108). As workers collaborate, this inarticulate dimension of human knowing is shared and encouraged throughout the organization.

Creativity Gaps

Sanchez-Bueno and Suarez-Gonzalez postulate that some new organizational forms may create a fundamental gap between the characteristics of the traditional organizational structures with the more innovative organizational form, and this gap may produce a non-innovative result (Sanchez-Bueno & Suarez-Gonzalez, 2010). This type of gap and non-innovative result actually happened to the Walt Disney Company. After Walt Disney's untimely death in 1966, his son-in-law assumes the CEO responsibilities and attempts to reorganize and realign the Walt Disney Company to make it more modern and up-to-date (Gabler, 2007). However, the innovative culture of the Disney Company begins to deteriorate after Walt's death because of a gap in the creative culture that Walt Disney developed and his successor changed (Thomas, 1994). As a reminder, the leadership of the Walt Disney Company also developed a program called "Traditions" to impart the importance of the Disney culture, heritage, values and policies as originally taught by Walt Disney to close the creative gap (Disney Institute, 2001).

Roy Disney Jr. (Walt's nephew) successfully led the Board of Directors to replace Walt Disney's son-in-law as the CEO with Michael Eisner who had to take the Traditions course on his first day of employment (Eisner, 1999). Eisner immediately re-established much of the organizational structure that Walt Disney used to enhance creativity. As Eisner began to merge Walt Disney's innovative culture with his own innovative culture and ideas, the Walt Disney Company expanded well beyond its previous boundaries in productivity and profit (Gabler, 2007). Eisner brought with him a vast background of experiences from his work at Paramount and ABC which he used to rebuild the Disney culture of innovation (Thomas, 1994). Eisner has come and gone at Disney, but the Traditions course is still a requirement for every cast member including the current Disney CEO (Gabler, 2007).

Pre-Emptive Crisis Management

In order to build and sustain an organizational culture dominated by creativity and innovation, learning organizations must effectively identify and mobilize the creative resources of their members before the intrusion of a crisis. Research at the London School of Economics define a learning organization as one that is able to change its behaviors/mind-sets as a result of experience, which may sound like an obvious statement, yet many organizations refuse to acknowledge certain truths or facts and repeat dysfunctional behaviors over and over again (Mitleton-Kelly, 2013). Tushman and O'Reilly claim that all too frequently organizational change is the product of crisis conditions, but the more successful firms do not wait until a crisis occurs before proactively developing/solving problems (Tushman & O'Reilly, 2002, p. 40).

Pro-active leadership development can help resolve a situation before a crisis can develop. Covey concludes that the ability to pause and then choose the response is the key to being proactive rather than reactive (Covey, 1989, p. 71). Creativity and innovation are critically important for organizations seeking to survive and thrive in today's highly turbulent business environments, and leadership development may represent one important key for unlocking this idle creative potential and enhancing overall organizational effectiveness (Houghton & DiLiello, 2010). One element of leadership development across learning organizations can be the emphasis upon everyone in the organization being creative. According to van Woerkum et al. from the Communication Management Group, Wageningen University, The Netherlands, being creative should be a part of an organization's everyday experiences, a component of normal meetings, and a reality for all members of an organization (van Woerkum, Aarts, & de Grip, 2007). Unlocking creativity and innovation before it is needed, will help learning organizations pre-empt a crisis situation.

The First Step

Perhaps the first step in the creative process could be to start asking "what's next". Gryskiewicz states that growth, creativity and stretching can be developed from the "what's next" question (Gryskiewicz, 1999, p. 52). Tushman and O'Reilly claim that all too frequently organizational change is the product of crisis conditions but the more successful firms do not wait until a crisis occurs before proactively developing or solving problems (Tushman & O'Reilly, 2002, p. 40). Bass contends that leaders need to be intuitive about what comes next and try to make it happen (Bass B. , 2008, p. 688). In order to build and sustain an organizational culture dominated by creativity, learning organizations must effectively identify and mobilize the creative resources of their members before the intrusion of a crisis. Developing a creative culture is not necessarily complex and most organizations can begin developing the creative culture at any time. Tushman and O'Reilly further explain that creativity only requires two main ingredients (Tushman & O'Reilly, 2002, p. 113):

- Support for Risk Taking
- Tolerance for Mistakes

Nadler and Tushman contend that much of the actual discussion on organizational structure does not show up on any formal charts, but it is centered in the ideologies, political alliances, collective self-images, webs of influence, career expectations, and patterns of behavior, which identifies what has come to be known as the "soft stuff" of organizational management and structure (Nadler & Tushman, 1997, p. 194). Creativity lies somewhere hidden in this "soft stuff" waiting to be discovered. This is also where leaders with a Biblical Christian Worldview are invaluable to an organization. From a Biblical Christian point of view, Romans 12:2 states that believers are not to be conformed to this world but transformed by the renewing of the mind. The Greek word for "conformed" is *suschematizo* and in this context means to model or pattern after a worldly appearance (Strong, 1981). The Greek word for "renewing" is the key to not being modeled or patterned after the world. This Greek word is *anakainosis* which means to renovate and produce a complete change for the better (Thayer, 1983). Discovering and utilizing combined creativity in the "soft stuff" of an organization will allow a person to renovate and produce a complete change for the better.

Creativity that Abides

Creativity is considered to be the source of new and competitive ideas through which an organization positions itself in its environment and, in rapidly changing conditions, organizations must meet the challenge of being capable of creating tomorrow's business while maintaining today's (van Woerkum, Aarts, & de Grip, 2007). Houghton and DiLiello define creativity as the process of forming novel, useful and appropriate ideas in order to solve problems and increase effectiveness, and view creativity as an individual or team level process; while innovation involves the successful implementation of creative ideas at the organizational level (Houghton & DiLiello, 2010). Although heavily influenced by their history and culture, organizations that develop an inter-dependence can transcend both when necessary, and they are able to explore the space of possibilities and find a different way of doing things, i.e., they are creative and innovative and can create something new (Mitleton-Kelly, 2013).

Education and technology are excellent keys for learning organizations to develop creativity. Tushman and O'Reilly notes that even Apple had to eventually expand and grow through education and technological advancements (Tushman & O'Reilly, 2002, p. 24). With tighter budgets and a global context, many educational and technological institutions are struggling to remain relevant for today and tomorrow. Canton states that innovation investments will be the key trend that will promote future leadership, education, quality of life, and global competitive advantages (Canton, 2006). The 2012 Horizon Report on higher education from the New Media Consortium identifies a timeline for technology implementation: one year or less for Mobile Apps and Tablet Computing; two to three years for game-based learning and learning analytics; four to five years for gesture-based computing (New Media Consortium, 2012). Additionally, the United Kingdom Government wants over 50% of their young people going to a university, and will rely on distance learning to meet this goal (Grocock, 2002). These trends and events would set the stage for non-traditional career paths led by creativity and technology innovations.

The global demand for higher education is likely to reach 160 million by 2025 with India and China becoming the two largest countries seeking higher education, and the demand is growing at the rate of 20% per annum in India (Gupta, 2008). Additionally, the New Media Consortium identifies the top 3 trends in higher education for 2012-2017 (New Media Consortium, 2012):

- People will expect to be able to work, learn, and study whenever and wherever they want and life in an increasingly busy world will produce more mobile students.
- Technologies will become increasingly cloud-based, as people are growing accustomed to a model of browser-based software that is device independent.
- The world of work will increasingly become more collaborative in nature and to facilitate more teamwork and group communication, projects will rely on tools such as wikis, Google Docs, and Skype.

According to Schneider and Littrell, many characteristics of the German way of management may be traced back to their national education system and its strengths in engineering, technical training and craft as well as German culture being less individualistic than the Anglo-Saxons; therefore the build-up of a long-term cooperative partnership between owners, managers and workers find a more fertile ground (Schneider & Littrell, 2003). Tushman and O'Reilly provide the success story of the turn-around of British Airways and conclude that their competitive advantage was the product of a cooperative shared culture throughout the organization that led to an increase in creativity and innovation (Tushman & O'Reilly, 2002, p. 33). To create an organization with a creative framework that abides requires a cooperative mindset to permeate throughout the entire organization. Everyone's involvement is paramount to producing a creative culture that abides. This type of creative thinking begins the process of developing a global strategic mindset.

Chapter 5
The Common Core of a Strategic Mindset

"Strategy without tactics is the slowest route to victory.
Tactics without strategy is the noise before defeat."
—Sun Tzu

"Would you tell me which way I ought to go from here?" asked Alice.
"That depends a good deal on where you want to get," said the Cat.
"I really don't care where" replied Alice.
"Then it doesn't much matter which way you go," said the Cat.
—Lewis Carroll

Strategic leadership is a topic that comes and goes in the course of the lives of most leaders. Innovative leaders are usually expected to provide answers and solutions to set the course for the future of their group or organization. Successful innovative leadership can be difficult to achieve because it does not follow a set pattern or form for each and every company or organization. However, there are some key elements that can be identified to assist leaders in developing a course of action in getting more of their people involved in innovative leadership, which will produce a strategic mindset for the people as a whole and the organization in particular. Two of these key elements are strategic thinking and strategic planning. Strategic, or simply strategy, becomes the common word for each of these key elements. Strategy is not a new concept. It has been around for literally thousands of years.

Sun Tzu and 2500 Years of Strategy

Strategy is a pattern that has demonstrated consistency in behavior over time and is applicable across all areas in industry (Mintzberg, Ahlstrand, & Lampel, 2005). Perhaps one of the oldest books ever written on the topic of strategy is ***The Art of War*** which is a 7000 word "book" originally written on bamboo strips around 500 B.C. by the master strategist Sun Tzu (Michaelson, 2001). Even after 2500 years of consistency over time, Sun Tzu is still relevant for military, government and business strategic leadership lessons. Many of the present day business strategies of organizations can be found in the foundational work of Sun Tzu (Oliver, 1999). A study in Hong Kong by Ho and Sculli conclude that the strategic guidance of Sun Tzu is not only applicable in a Chinese management structure but in all studies of strategy covered in management science (Ho & Sculli, 1998).

However, strategy is a difficult word to define because strategy is always used within a context of competition and change which can best be described like nailing Jell-O™ to a wall (Marren, 2010). Mintzberg et al. identify five definitions related to strategy and determine that strategy is a word that is defined one way but used in a different manner; he also produced 10 schools of thought on strategy (Mintzberg, Ahlstrand, & Lampel, 2005):

1. The Design School, which sees strategic management as a process of attaining a fit between the internal capabilities and external possibilities of an organization.
2. The Planning School, which extols the virtues of formal strategic planning and arms itself with SWOT analyses and checklists.
3. The Positioning School, heavily influenced by the ideas of Michael Porter, which stresses that strategy depends on the positioning of the firm in the market and within its industry.
4. The Entrepreneurial School, which emphasizes the central role played by the leader.
5. The Cognitive School, which looks inwards into the minds of strategists.
6. The Learning School, which sees strategy as an emergent process —strategies emerge as people come to learn about a situation as

well as their organization's capability of dealing with it.

7. The Power School, which views strategy emerging out of power games within the organization and outside it.
8. The Cultural School, which views strategy formation as a process rooted in the social force of culture.
9. The Environmental School, which believes that a firm's strategy depends on events in the environment and the company's reaction to them.
10. The Configuration School, which views strategy as a process of transforming the organization—it describes the relative stability of strategy, interrupted by occasional and dramatic leaps to new ones.

De Kluyver defines strategy as the act of positioning a company for competitive advantage by focusing on unique ways to create value for customers (de Kluyver & Pearce II, 2012). Innovation leadership would greatly benefit from the study of strategic thinking and strategic planning by Sun Tzu and even Clausewitz.

Clausewitz

Many times, strategy indicates a military context. Military leaders have been using the strategic teachings of Clausewitz since his widow published his famous book ***On War*** in 1832 and no true strategist can fully understand the complexities of strategy without delving into Clausewitz (The Strategy Institute of the Boston Consulting Group, 2001). According to Oliver, many of the present day business strategies of organizations can be found in the foundational work of Clausewitz and Sun Tzu (Oliver, 1999). Clausewitz may be best known for his "fog of war" concept, which is used to describe the uncertainty in situational awareness activities experienced by participants in military operations but would also apply to uncertainty in any strategic endeavor.

Strategic Thinking

Strategy has also been defined as a learning process and a strategic mindset can be defined as a way of thinking about how to craft and implement that learning process (Hughes & Beatty, 2005). As more people across the organization get involved, sustainability becomes a greater possibility. The world is becoming increasingly "flat", which means that to effectively conduct business in this new world it will require a different kind of leader; a leader who will not only have to be generally effective in the traditional skills expected, but also with additional knowledge, skills and, above all, a mindset to navigate through the complexities brought on by moving beyond one's traditional borders (Cohen S. L., 2010).

Successful leaders working in complex, ambiguous or chaotic environments think more strategically than less successful leaders in those same environments. Three cognitive processes associated with strategic thinking can be identified as potential distinguishers between successful leaders and less successful leaders: reflection, systems thinking, and reframing (Pisapia, Reyes-Guerra, & Coukos-Semmel, 2005).

Reflection

Reflection is a cognitive skill that involves careful consideration of any belief or practice that promotes understanding of situations and then applying newly gained knowledge to these situations (Pisapia, Reyes-Guerra, & Coukos-Semmel, 2005). It relies on subjecting evidence, perception and experience to critical scrutiny in order to make sense and meaning of situations prior to weaving the thinking into a theory of practice. By reflecting on both successes and failures, leaders begin to unpack the assumptions and values that lie beneath rules, regulations and processes in work and everyday life. This constant effort of reevaluation and interpretation is an integral part of how leaders make sense of situations.

Systems Thinking

Systems thinking rests on the notion that the "whole is greater than the parts." In systems thinking the whole is primary and the parts are secondary. When developing a global strategic mindset, this level of strategic thinking focuses on the big picture concept. In other words, start with the forest as a whole and then spiral down into the individual trees. Systems thinking are invaluable in a cause and effect analogy. This is especially important in strategic thinking as it pertains to future development and insight, which allows modeling a change in the system in order to predict a series of outcomes.

Reframing

Leaders frame and place all situations in a context. Framing is a cognitive process that helps us gather and organize information and create knowledge. It involves sorting and interpreting the meaning of new information, events, and experiences. Framing imposes assumptions and provides a language for analysis of behavior in which certain aspects of situations are chosen to be considered and interpreted. Reframing has grown in importance since the mid-1980s and Morgan contends that situations and/or problems could be framed and reframed in different ways allowing new kinds of solutions to emerge (Morgan, 1997, p. 337).

Strategic Thinking Leads to Strategic Planning

While the first element or component of developing a strategic mindset involves strategic thinking, it also leads to the second component, which is strategic planning. Even Sun Tzu made reference to a Director of Strategic Planning (Michaelson, 2001). Strategic thinking and strategic planning are interrelated processes and both are necessary for effective strategic management (Heracleos, 1998). However, strategic planning comes after strategic thinking and involves writing or updating a written plan. It requires the clear setting of goals and objectives which are then used to provide the organization with its core priorities as well as a set of written guidelines for virtually all day-to-day managerial decisions (Harrison, 1995). Mintzberg concludes that strategic planning establishes and formularizes systems and procedures (Mintzberg, 1994).

Producing a Strategic Mindset

In every organization, leaders struggle with meeting the demands of a globalized society and local constraints. During the latter half of the last century, leadership challenges were largely framed in the cold war context that created a stabilizing and linear notion of change. Today, the stability of all institutions is challenged by the rapid speed of change driven by globalization, shifting populations, integration of advanced information, and communications technologies which diminishes the impact of time, space, and distance. This transition from the modern industrial age to the postmodern information age with its accompanying complexity is creating a profound challenge for all organizational leaders (Pisapia, Reyes-Guerra, & Coukos-Semmel, 2005).

In today's globally connected society, traditional leaders and leadership structures are becoming a thing of the past. Many organizations are becoming flatter and leadership styles more flexible. According to Bennis, today's globally connected organizations are evolving into federations, networks, clusters, cross-functional teams, temporary systems, ad hoc task forces, lattices, modules, matrices—almost anything but pyramids with their obsolete top-down leadership (Bennis, 1999). A globally connected society requires globally connected leaders. McCall and Hollenbeck identified seven competencies for a global strategic leader (McCall Jr. & Hollenbeck, 2002, p. 36):

- Open Minded and Flexible in Thought and Tactics
- Cultural Interest and Sensitivity
- Able to Deal with Complexity
- Resilient, Resourceful, Optimistic and Energetic
- Honesty and Integrity
- Stable Personal Life
- Value-Added Technical or Business Skills

Time and experience become the true measures of these competencies for innovative leaders. This becomes a greater challenge for globally connected leaders and organizations. However, starting with these seven competencies is a step in the right direction.

Synthesis of Strategic Thinking and Planning

Strategic thinking and planning involves synthesis, which encourages intuitive, innovative and creative thinking (Mintzberg, Ahlstrand, & Lampel, 2005). From the field of education, Benjamin Bloom identifies six levels of thinking, which are commonly called Bloom's Taxonomy of Learning. Synthesis and evaluation are the fifth and sixth level of Bloom's Taxonomy. According to Bloom, "synthesis" is the ability to put ideas together, propose plans, form solutions, and create new information; whereas, in the "evaluation" stage, the thinker is able to make choices, select, evaluate and make judgments about information and situations (Bloom, 1971). Bloom further contends that in order to get to this level, cognitive thought processes must go through the other four levels which consist of knowledge, comprehension, application and analysis (Bloom, 1971).

In other words, for strategic thinking to work at the synthesis level of thinking, the accumulation of facts and knowledge must lead to a comprehensive understanding which leads to an application and analysis process. Then, the level of synthesis in the strategic thinking process can begin. Strategic planning is closely related to Bloom's evaluation level where choices are selected, acted upon, and then evaluated. Hughes and Beatty emphasize that strategic thinking and strategic planning lead to strategic acting and strategic influence (Hughes & Beatty, 2005). This thought carries out Bloom's evaluation level of thinking. This type of processing becomes more circular than linear. Evaluations are made which may lead back to the need for more facts and knowledge, and the cycle of continuous improvement continues.

Strategic thinking is focused on conceptualizing alternatives and choices through vision and innovation. It leads to the clear setting of goals and objectives which are then used to provide the organization with its core priorities as well as a set of written guidelines for virtually all day-to-day managerial decisions (Harrison, 1995). Where strategic thinking is conceptual of the vision, strategic planning involves writing the vision. Habakkuk 2:2 provides the instruction to write the vision and make it plain (Spirit Filled Life Bible (NKJV), 1991). While it may seem easy to confuse the difference between thinking and planning, the distinction can be found in that thinking is based on conceptualizing and planning is based upon the writing of goals and objectives to be followed. Thinking precedes planning and planning makes the thinking process actionable. This type of planning works for countries as well as organizations.

Global Use of Strategic Thinking

All countries including developing countries can benefit from strategic thinking. Many global organizations struggle with finding answers to the questions about the needs of the present and what to do about the needs of tomorrow. Mintzberg et al. state that one of the seven deadly sins of strategic planning is to neglect the organizational and cultural requirements of strategy (Mintzberg, Ahlstrand, & Lampel, 2005). Like organizations, successful countries and cultures are dependent upon strategic leadership and strategic thinking. Hughes and Beatty identify five strategic thinking competencies that can be used for organizations or countries: scanning, visioning, reframing, making common sense and systems thinking (Hughes & Beatty, 2005).

Leadership of a country in a complex world that is ever changing and becoming more competitive can especially benefit from the systems thinking component. Palaima and Skaržauskiene reported in the Baltic Journal of Management that effective decision making in a world of growing dynamic complexity requires leaders to become systems thinkers in order to develop tools to understand the structures of complex systems that make up in the inner workings of any culture (Palaima & Skaržauskiene, 2010). Some countries are still struggling to make adaptation to a global environment surrounded by complex systems. The Sudan, especially in the Darfur region, provides an example of a failed state due to poor governance, institutional failures in the country as whole, the failure of economic institutions and the breakdown of local institutions (Madichie, 2011). With tribal factions and local juntas fighting for control in the failed state of Sudan, the concept of strategic thinking is not at work. A stable government may be the first step in order to begin building a nation with the five components of strategic thinking. This is also true for organizations. When an organization is in crisis mode, strategic thinking is usually one of the first items dropped from consideration. It is difficult to plan for long-term goals and objectives when the ship is sinking.

According to Yaprak and Sheldon, political risk assessment must be considered, and integrating political risk management into the corporate planning function of a multinational firm is required, in order to produce a successful strategic plan for investment into a country and identified several events in the Middle East and North Africa to demonstrate the volatility of global political currents of the day (Yaprak & Sheldon, 1984). It is of interest to note that even though this article was written in 1984, many of the same type of events are currently taking place in those same areas today.

Frynas references that many business managers and strategic planners identify the political instability in Africa as a key obstacle to its economic development (Frynas, 1998). Additionally, the United Nations identifies that in many developing countries one of the primary challenges for strategic planning and growth is the need for political stability (United Nations, 2006). Mintzberg et al. conclude that strategy formation is a process of social interaction based upon the beliefs and understandings that are shared by the members of an organization (Mintzberg, Ahlstrand, & Lampel, 2005). Successful social interaction to develop a strategic plan is difficult at best in a dictatorship regime or a politically unstable government/ environment. While political stability may not be the primary factor in a countries' strategic plan development, political risk assessment is an important component of a country or cultural group developing a successful strategic plan.

According to Hans Finzel, failure to focus on the future is one of the top ten mistakes that leaders make and concludes that vision is an effective leader's chief preoccupation (Finzel, 1994). Bennis identifies that the key to a leader moving into the future is to develop a mental image that articulates a view of a realistic yet credible and attractive future for the organization (Bennis W. G., 1992). Sanders determines that pictures and images have the power to convey content and meaning and that visualization is the key to both insight and foresight which leads to the next revolution in strategic thinking and planning (Sanders T. I., 1998). While different countries or cultures may vary in the implementation of the strategic plan, visual thinking and producing an achievable vision would seem to be a vital step during the strategic thinking process. Oster concludes that a vision which is extraordinarily expansive and even unreasonable—many would say impossible—is the key to producing successful innovation (Oster, 2011). Not all strategic plans lead to innovation. Visual thinking can still be used in the innovation process. The ability to see beyond the realistic and peer into the impossible or near impossible requires a leader to push beyond the edge to see what may be out there.

Go Global Act Local

A global mindset is vital for innovative leaders of today. One option for global leaders to create environments that facilitate and encourage employee creativity could be to look for local experts. Von Krough et al. state that managers should assign local experts or spokespeople to the knowledge that is dispatched (Von Krogh, Ichijo, & Nonaka, 2000, p. 218). Global leaders must also consider local cultural components. While the Apostle Paul may not have been present with Jesus when He gave the original Apostles the Great Commission, Luke's record in Acts 1:8 typifies Paul's commission to be a witness in Jerusalem, in all Judea and Samaria and to the ends of the earth (HCSB, 2010). Paul's vision of the future was "to go." To be a global leader requires the leader to go. Paul understood this concept. He is credited with writing approximately half of the New Testament, but his greater achievement may have been that he actually traveled to all the places to which he wrote letters. It is one thing to write letters; however, it is another thing to have traveled to all those locations before writing the letters. To engage with people of other cultures requires the leader to travel and stay in those areas in order to learn about the people, their cultures and ideologies.

According to Robbins, the Ideological Texture begins with people, and he defines ideology as an integrated system of beliefs, assumptions, and values (Robbins, 1996, p. 96). DeSilva identifies that Ideological Texture recognizes that a text is not just a vehicle for ideas but rather a vehicle by which the author hopes to achieve a certain goal (DeSilva, 2004, p. 25). Luke starts off Acts 1:8 with his version of the Great Commission and then provides substantial detail about Paul's efforts to fulfill that commission through his travels. Horsley and Silberman ascertain that when Paul was in Antioch he quickly becomes one of Antioch's most energetic and outspoken organizers, and then he is launched into the world (Horsley & Silberman, 2002, p. 129). Energy and passion are vital for organizational leaders to reach across cultures and build a community. While complex and more gelatinous than Jell-O™, strategic thinking and strategic planning will allow innovative leaders to build the core competency of a strategic mindset.

Chapter 6
The Common Core of Redesign

"Never doubt that a small group of thoughtful,
committed, citizens can change the world. Indeed,
it is the only thing that ever has."
—Margaret Mead

"The only person who likes change is a wet baby."
—Mark Twain

Change is everywhere. The status quo no longer exists. Many formerly successful businesses and organizations are closing their doors on a regular basis. Successful organizations of today must keep moving forward looking for new competitive advantages. Many times, what is missing about the dynamics of change is the big picture context in which decisions are made (Sanders T. I., 1998, p. 11). Strategic leadership helps provide that big picture context for organizations. As stated, Hughes and Beatty define strategic leadership as when people think, act, and influence in ways that promote a sustainable competitive advantage for the organization (Hughes & Beatty, 2005, p. 9). People and sustainable become key words in this definition. Future successful organizations need to get more of their people involved in strategic leadership at all organizational levels and functions. As more people begin to see opportunities to work in specific ways that affect the direction and momentum of the organization, they begin to take ownership and leadership of their particular area. The more that people get involved, the more sustainable the strategic leadership plan becomes especially during a time of change and redesign.

Change and Motivation

In today's turbulent environment of organizations, change has become synonymous with standard business practices involving long-term organizational ends which must be reformulated on an ongoing basis; however, the largest barrier to change is not changes to technologies or work processes but changes that involve people (Appelbaum, St-Pierre, & Glavas, 1998). Motivation becomes a key component in enabling changes that involve people inside an organization. If people want the change or at least understand the need for change, there is much less resistance. Deming identifies two types of motivation: intrinsic, which involves the natural inclination to learn and the desire to be around other people whereas extrinsic involves external forces in building self-esteem and motivation (Deming, 1994). However, Deming also concludes that some extrinsic motivation can be used to help build self-esteem, but total submission to external motivation leads to the destruction of the individual (Deming, 1994).

Being part of a successful group is a motivational plan that empowers the people in that group to reach out and recruit others. After all, everybody likes to be on the winning side. However, occasions exist where top-down directed change has met with resistance to produce unfavorable outcomes. For example, the United States Air Force has an unpaid civilian auxiliary component called the Civil Air Patrol (CAP), which used to wear Air Force (AF) uniforms when performing search and rescue missions looking for downed aircraft. After some CAP members did not properly wear the uniform, the AF instituted a top-down uniform change making the CAP uniform more distinct from the AF uniform. However, CAP members affirm that they were motivated solely by a desire to perform the CAP's mission and not motivated by wearing AF uniforms, quit and withdrew commitment. Cheng claims that the AF's misunderstanding of volunteer motivation and the symbolism of organizational uniforms led to a dysfunctional organizational change (Cheng, 1998).

Business processes change over time and in order to reflect new and emerging business needs, the organizational structure often needs to be redesigned. This includes the organizational chart, positional changes, job descriptions, career paths, succession plans, etc. Some organizational redesign is compartmental in an organization while other redesigns are for the organization as a whole. It is one thing to pull out a piece of paper and design a new organizational chart. It is quite another thing to build the right organization for the right reasons, staff it appropriately, and then determine what is required to make that new organization work. Organizations often redesign themselves to unlock latent value and typically pay a great deal of attention to the form of the new design because a successfully implemented redesign is supposed to generate value as well as increasing competitive advantage (Ghislanzoni, Heidari-Robinson, & Jermiin, December 2010). The concept of managing change can also be called redesign, and a successful redesign starts with a well-developed strategic plan.

Redesign Change: A Competitive Advantage

Hughes and Beatty contend that strategic thinking is the collection, interpretation, generation, and evaluation of information and ideas in order to create a competitive advantage for the group or organization (Hughes & Beatty, 2005, p. 44). Businesses where creative thinking is not valued and nurtured will struggle to compete with more visionary enterprises because strategic leadership requires creative thinking and innovation in order to produce effective results (Vaitheeswaran, 2008). Mintzberg's first school of thought is the Design School which sees strategic management as a process of attaining a fit between the internal capabilities and external possibilities of an organization (The Executive Fast Track, 2012):

- This school sees strategy formation as a process of conception.
- Approach: Clear and unique strategies are formulated in a deliberate process. In this process, the internal situation of the organization is matched to the external situation of the environment.
- Basis: Architecture as a metaphor.
- In short: Fit! "Establish Fit!"
- Contributions: Order. Reduced ambiguity. Simplicity. Useful in relatively stable environments. It supports strong, visionary leadership.

- Limitations: Simplification may distort reality. Strategy has many variables and is inherently complex. Bypassing learning. Inflexible. Weak in fast changing environment. There is the risk of resistance (not-invented-here behavior).
- Typical/compare: SWOT Analysis I Ashridge Mission Model

Additionally, organizational growth requires companies to closely monitor their return on investments and return on assets with the Economic Value Added (EVA) and the Market Value Added measures. Lehn and Makhija identified that EVA is employed by a large number of firms, including Coca-Cola, AT&T, Quaker Oats, Eli Lilly, Georgia Pacific, and Tenneco and, unlike traditional accounting measures of performance, EVA attempts to measure the value that firms create or destroy by subtracting a capital charge from the returns they generate on invested capital (Lehn & Makhija, 1996). Creating and identifying value is vital to the success and growth of any company.

Redesign: Innovation

Change brings about restructuring and reorganization: change to the working relationships, change to roles and tasks—plus the personal change relating to all of those organizational changes. Reorganizations are hard work. Organizational redesign can be a traumatic experience for all involved, and may falter as managers lose focus or try to compromise on tough decisions. To be successful, a redesign must be based on sound organizational analysis and an agreed-to, implementable long-term business strategy. The skills that come into play to help formulate and guide future strategy are not just learned from textbooks; they are developed over years of exposure to a broad variety of corporate situations in a wide range of industrial, market and geographical contexts. These qualitative shifts revolutionize our ways of thinking, entailing a radical overhaul of concepts, attitudes and values. It follows that education and training must also change, to meet the demands of a culture in which innovation becomes the universal norm (Garavan & Deegan, 1995). Ashkenas et al. conclude that success factors in the twenty-first century include speed, flexibility, integration and innovation, which is in addition to the traditional success factors of size, role, definition, specialization and control (Ashkenas, Ulrich, Jick, & Kerr, 2002, p. xviii).

Redesign: Seven Factors

With tighter budgets and a global context, many organizations are struggling to stay relevant for today and tomorrow. Innovation may become the key to what many organizational structures and facilities will look like in the future. According to Oster, innovation is defined as the intentional development of a specific product, service, idea, process or environment for the creation of value (Oster, 2011, p. 16). For organizations to remain relevant in an ever-changing society, the value of the product needs to increase. The need to increase product value can lead to structural redesign. However, knowing when to redesign becomes a vital component for the future of organizational development. Nadler and Tushman identify seven factors that push organizations toward redesign (Nadler & Tushman, 1997, pp. 207-216):

1. Patterns of Industry Evolution
    a. Stage 1: Emerging Industries which represents the early days of an organization. These organizations learn from trial and error and quickly innovate on the run.
    b. Stage 2: Evolving Industries represents a time of increased demand. With increasing complexity, size and volume comes the need for more professional management than the original entrepreneurial organization could provide.
    c. Stage 3: Mature Industries occurs as demands level off, which may result in the basis of competition shifts. These organizations become firmly focused on cost, efficiencies and process innovation.
2. Discontinuous Change: Periods of disequilibrium that tend to cause a radical shift away from the status quo.
3. New Structural Materials: Emerges over time leading to the development of new organizational architectures, and as growth accelerates many organizations adopt the new structure which compels other organizations to, at least, give serious thought to revamping their own design. While innovation may weave in and out of many, if not all, of these factors, it becomes a critical piece of the new structural materials factor. New advances in technology, information, and organizational architecture emerge over time and lead to the development of new organizational structures.

4. Organizational Growth: As organizations grow they don't just get bigger, they get more complex as expansion inevitably brings more volume, more differentiation, more specialization, a broader range of offerings to customers, and new geographic locations.
5. The Success Syndrome: Occurs when companies sow the seed of their own failure in a self-destructive pattern which can occur as organizations increase in size and form bureaucracies to impose rigid controls at the expense of speed and flexibility.
6. Management Succession: The installation of a new CEO often provides the stimulus for major redesign efforts and generally falls into one of the four following categories:
    a. Responding to an inherited crisis
    b. Making a personal statement
    c. Pursuing a new strategy
    d. Shaking up the place
7. Organizational Mutation: At most organizations, there are always some design experiments in the works. Every so often, one of these innovations catches on and, in turn, influences the larger organization design. At these junctures, the gradual evolution of the organization's architecture is jolted by a sudden mutation that accelerates change or steers it in a new direction.

Redesign: World Vision

World Vision is a great example of a not-for-profit humanitarian organization that is reliant upon a unique organizational structure for success and exhibits the Organizational Growth factor. According to Foreman, World Vision International is the current organizational structure of the World Vision Partnership which operates today as a federation of interdependent national offices with three different levels of central control, which are (Foreman, 1999):

- National offices which are under strong central control and are registered in the host country as a branch of World Vision International.
- Intermediate stage national offices that have their own board but have agreed to seek approval from World Vision International for critical management decisions.

- Interdependently national registered offices that are autonomous in internal decision but are expected to coordinate with World Vision International and are bound to the Covenant of Partnership.

The idea for World Vision began in the late 1940's when a war correspondent, Dr. Bob Pierce, was sent to China and his heart was broken due to the need of a single little girl whom he started supporting by sending a monthly amount of money to a local missionary for her care (Irvine, 1996, p. 187). From this meager beginning, World Vision has grown to work in over 90 countries, with an estimated 40,000 employees and volunteers as well as annual revenue close to 3 billion dollars (World Vision, 2012). A solitary encounter with a single individual has produced a global outreach organization.

Redesign: Disney

Another great success story of the modern era is the Walt Disney Company. This example demonstrates many of these seven factors; especially, the Organizational Growth and Management Succession factors. The success of Disney is well known with millions of people visiting Disney theme parks on 3 continents, 4 cruise ships, countless movies. The Walt Disney Company had annual revenue of US $36 billion in 2010 (sec.gov, 2010). What is not as well known is that prior to moving to California, Walt Disney started an animation studio in Kansas City called Laugh-O-Gram Studio in 1922, and had as many as 4 animators working for him including life-long Disney animator, Ub Iwerks (Gabler, 2007, p. 73). However, Walt Disney was never good at handling money so that studio went bankrupt, and Walt Disney moved to California to start Walt Disney Productions with his brother, Roy Disney, taking over as the money manager (Thomas, 1994, p. 75). After successfully starting Walt Disney Studios, Walt Disney was asked about his key to success; a good failure was his quick response (Thomas, 1994, p. 77). Walt Disney was able to take what he had learned from his failed business venture in Kansas and use that knowledge to make adjustments for the Walt Disney Studios in California.

While, it may be easier to learn from successes, perhaps the greatest amount of learning can come from failures. From their research in Sweden,

Politis and Gabrielsson conclude that previous start up experience and the experience from closing down a business are associated with a more positive attitude towards failure (Gabrielsson & Politis, 2009). Walt Disney was well known to state that "It is good to have a hard failure while you are young because it teaches you so much. For one thing it makes you aware that such a thing can happen to anybody, and once you've lived through the worst, you're never quite as vulnerable afterwards (Smith, 2001, p. 32)." After the death of Walt Disney, the leadership of the Walt Disney Company developed a program called "Traditions" which imparts the importance of Disney culture, heritage, values and policies as originally taught by Walt Disney, and part of that class still teaches Walt Disney's belief about having a hard failure (Disney Institute, 2001, p. 32). Mintzberg et al. would call the strategic approach that Walt Disney used as the Entrepreneurial School which sees strategy formation as a visionary process and identifies the CEO as the architect of the strategy (Mintzberg, Ahlstrand, & Lampel, p. 104). After Walt Disney unexpectedly died in 1966, the leadership of the Walt Disney Company developed a program called "Traditions" to impart the importance of the Disney culture, heritage, values and policies as originally taught by Walt Disney (Disney Institute, 2001, p. 84). With the Traditions class firmly in place and currently taught to every employee (called cast members) on their first day at work, including their new CEO, the visionary process of Walt Disney continues even after a hard failure.

Many large organizations will initiate a redesign by making a CEO change in order to recover an organization. The Walt Disney Company is also an example of a large organization that changed the CEO in order to change the culture of innovation of the company. The innovative culture of the Disney Company begins to deteriorate after Walt's death (Thomas, 1994, p. 354). In order to facilitate a corporate redesign, Roy Disney Jr. (Walt's nephew) successfully leads the Board of Directors to replace Walt Disney's son-in-law as the CEO with Michael Eisner (Eisner, 1998, p. 146).

Redesign: Front-Back Hybrid Organization

As organizations grow and expand to the global arena, developing a redesign that fits the business processes as well as integrating other cultures becomes complex. One redesign that could benefit these types of organizations is the Front-Back Hybrid Organization design. Galbraith ascertains that this type of design provides two line organizations: one focused on the customer (the front end) while a second line focuses on products (the back end) with the objective in all cases being to achieve customer focus and responsiveness concurrent with global scale economies (Galbraith J. R., 2000, p. 238). This type of design allows organizations to develop customer-focused methodologies while allowing the organization to expand. Organizational growth places a new demand for global leaders. Black et al. identify that 85 percent of firms feel that they do not have an adequate number of global leaders and 67 percent feel that that the global leaders they do have need additional skills and knowledge in order to meet the growth of the organization (Black, Morrison, & Gregersen, 1999, p. 185). The development of this type of redesign model can be used to enable companies to manage their growth expansion and grow global leaders through the development process. When the front end is based on countries, the objective is to achieve the elusive global-local combination, which results from resolving the management challenge of effectively linking the customer front with the product back (Galbraith J. R., 2000, p. 238).

Redesign Process

Organizational redesign can come from any of Nadler and Tushman's seven factors; however, it is also imperative to study organizations that have already been through the process. The McKinsey Quarterly completed a survey from November 9 to November 19, 2010, and received responses from 2,525 executives, of whom 1,890 had been through an organizational redesign in the past five years; this survey, which represented the full range of regions, industries, functional specialties, tenures, and company sizes, identified the top 12 reasons why their organizations underwent a redesign (Ghislanzoni, Heidari-Robinson, & Jermiin, December 2010):

1. Responding to growth, 18 percent
2. Cutting costs, 12 percent
3. Moving to a best practice model, 12 percent
4. Introducing change, 10 percent

5. Reducing complexity, 8 percent
6. Increasing revenues, 8 percent
7. Fulfilling a new leader's desire to make changes, 7 percent
8. Responding to a crisis, 7 percent
9. Integrating previous acquisitions, 6 percent
10. Facilitating a merger, 6 percent
11. Responding to regulatory pressure, 2 percent
12. Improving risk management, 1 percent

As organizations analyze their redesign process, it is vital to understand the need for a redesign and then develop a strategic plan that will enable the success of a redesign. Many companies have successfully completed an organizational redesign and other companies have failed at redesign. Global leaders need to know the reasons for redesign success and failures. Additionally, knowledge and experience with successful redesign models like the Front-Back Hybrid model becomes even more valuable. Organizations are looking for global leaders that can effectively and productively create organizational redesigns for the future.

Chapter 7
The Common Core of Trust

"He who does not trust enough, Will not be trusted."
—Lao Tzu

"Never be afraid to trust an unknown future to a known God."
—Corrie ten Boom

"The day soldiers stop bringing you their problems is the day you have stopped leading them. They have lost their confidence that you can help them or concluded that you do not care. Either case is a failure of leadership."
—Colin Powell

Leadership is as much about who we are as what we do. This is especially vital in building cross-culture relationships in those we lead. One of the core ingredients in "whom we are" is the concept of trust. Bennis identifies that one of the core competencies of leadership is that leaders generate and sustain trust (Bennis, 1999). Elmuti and Kathawala conclude that a lack of trust will always lead to a leadership failure as well as a failure in strategic alliances (Elmuti & Kathawala, 2001). Leadership style and focus will also affect trust. Joseph and Winston determine that perceptions of servant leadership correlated positively with leader trust and determine that organizations perceived as servant-led exhibited higher levels of leader trust than organizations perceived as non-servant-led (Joseph & Winston, 2005).Trust is a major factor in organizational success, and any organization would benefit from that type of design. However, designing an organization to instill and develop trust can be challenging.

Simons describes that perceptions parallel behavioral integrity as antecedents of trust and identifies that research on organizational behavior identifies that inconsistency between words and deeds decreases trust as well as noting how lies and distortions decrease trust, while undistorted communication reinforces trust (Simons, 1999). Distrust and ineffective communication can quickly dissolve into cynicism. According to Henry and Richard Blackaby, cynical leaders cultivate cynical followers when they are constantly criticizing others thereby modeling a critical spirit for others to follow, and it is imperative that leaders not allow themselves to be consumed by a cynical spirit (Blackaby & Blackaby, 2001). If leaders do not earn the people's trust by living a life of integrity and being true to their values, people simply will not follow them too far.

People First

According to Sendjaya and Pekerti, trust is a mutual benefit derived from a covenantal relationship, and the leader as well as the follower has to build a trust relationship (Sendjaya & Pekerti, 2010). Pfeffer contends that putting people first is a key strategy to develop trust for successful businesses (Pfeffer, 1998, p. 17). Air Force General Hal Hornburg was well known in the military for his philosophy of leading, which was People First—Mission Always (Air Force Times, 2004). While this phrase was not original with General Hornburg, the Air Force has been promoting this emphasis on people for many years. However, this type of leadership is not unique just to the Air Force. Army Major General Reuben Jones uses this same phrase in emphasizing the need for Army leaders to balance their lives (Jones, 2010). In addition to this type of leadership spreading across US military cultures, some international coalition partners are also calling upon this type of leadership. On 31 July 2011, Air Chief Marshal Norman Anil Kumar Browne became India's 23rd Chief of the Air Staff. Air Chief Marshal Browne noted that the Indian Air Force was on the verge of transforming itself into a "potent strategic force" and unveiled his "People First Mission Always" vision for the force (The Hindu, 2011).

Higher trust levels build stronger ties between the leader and the follower (Sendjaya & Pekerti, 2010). Trust becomes the substance holding people together in a group or organization. Trust is a value that should transcend cultures and build strong relationships for innovative leaders. Bennis identified four competencies of the new leader that will determine the future success for organizations (Bennis, 1999):

- The new leader understands and practices the power of appreciation. They are connoisseurs of talent, and more curators than creators.
- The new leader keeps reminding people of what's important.
- The new leader and the led are intimate allies.
- The new leader generates and sustains trust.

Elements of Trust

According to Von Krogh et al., every encounter with another person establishes some degree of trust, which compensates for the lack of knowledge about that person (Von Krogh, Ichijo, & Nonaka, 2000, p. 49). Kouzes and Posner determine that trusting other people encourages their trust, but distrusting others makes them lose confidence; leaders benefit by clearly communicating trust and accessibility to their constituents (Kouzes & Posner, 1993). This type of interaction requires leaders to build upon strong levels of trust and credibility. Open lines of communication are vital links to build the levels of trust and credibility required for global leadership. Bell identifies three elements of trust making (Bell C. R., 2002):

- Trust starts with authenticity
- Trust depends on credibility
- Trust is enabled through communication

Schein contends that levels of trust and openness across various boundaries are likely to be a cultural issue; therefore, it is best to start with a heterogeneous group and let the group experience the extent to which certain areas of communication are or are not inhibited by the presence of others (Schein, 1997). It is vital that leaders openly show their trust in their followers in order to allow them the freedom to release their creativity and innovation. Winston and Patterson claim that trust and credibility work together in a successful leader-follower relationship (Winston & Patterson, 2006).

Trustworthiness

The "trustworthiness" of leaders is closely tied to their ethical commitment. According to Robbins' sacred texture, ethics concerns the responsibility of humans to think and act in special ways in both extraordinary and ordinary circumstances (Robbins, 1996, p. 129). Bass expounds that ideologically inspired amoral theories are being preached in many business schools and management development programs across the country, which free future organizational leaders from any sense of moral responsibility for their decisions as well as encouraging, rather than inhibiting, this type of opportunistic behavior (Bass B., 2008). Simons determines that the challenge of maintaining behavioral integrity is critical for the development of trust as well as being vital for successful change efforts (Simons, 1999). This type of motivation requires leaders to build upon strong levels of trust and credibility.

Burns defines a transformational leader as one who raises the followers' level of consciousness about the importance and value of outcomes and how to effectively reach them (Burns, 1978, p. 142). Trust is required to produce these outcomes. Understanding the cultural environment is vital to leaders building relationships and earning trust. Woolfe states that if leaders have not earned the people's trust by constantly keeping their word and being true to their values, then it doesn't matter how noble or worthwhile the cause because people will not follow them too far (Woolfe, 2002). Developing relationships based upon trust will be vital to lead successful organizations in today's globally connected environment.

Trust and the Early Church

The early development of the church as an organizational structure provides an excellent example of how a "new" start-up organization can grow and expand through the use of trust. The church age begins in the Book of Acts, which does not specifically identify the author; however, Luke historically has been considered the author. Since Acts does not mention the fall of Jerusalem in AD 70 nor Paul's death, it is logical to date the writing of the Book of Acts to around 62 AD (Hayford, 1995, p. 327).

In this book, Luke tells the story of the early church within the framework of geographical, political, and historical detail. At an Upper Room prayer meeting described in Acts chapter one, 120 believers gather in a trusted environment, which is described as being in one accord, to usher in the Holy Spirit that Jesus promised in order to birth the Christian church. Acts 1:14 identifies a key Scripture to start the Christian era "These all continued with one accord in prayer and supplication, with the women and Mary the mother of Jesus, and with His brothers (Spirit Filled Life Bible (NKJV), 1991)." The phrase translated "one accord" is the Greek word *homothumadon* (Strong, 1981).

One Accord: Unity and Harmony

This phrase identifies an important characteristic of the early church. Thayer defines *homothumadon* as being in one mind or unanimously united in purpose (Thayer, 1983, p. 445). In addition to Acts 1:14, this concept of unity and harmony is a continuing trait of the early church with each other as well as with the Lord as noted in the following Scriptures (Spirit Filled Life Bible (NKJV), 1991):

- Acts 2:1, when the Day of Pentecost had fully come, they were all with one accord in one place
- Acts 2:46, so continuing daily with one accord in the temple, and breaking bread from house to house, they ate their food with gladness and simplicity of heart
- Acts 4:24, so when they heard that, they raised their voice to God with one accord and said: "Lord, You are God, who made heaven and earth and the sea, and all that is in them
- Acts 5:12, and through the hands of the apostles many signs and wonders were done among the people. And they were all with one accord in Solomon's Porch
- Acts 15:25, it seemed good to us, being assembled with one accord, to send chosen men to you with our beloved Barnabas and Paul

The Greek word, *homothumadon*, is used 12 times in the New Testament with 11 of those times being in the Book of Acts (Wigram, 1979, p. 530).

Social and Cultural Texture

These Scriptures from Acts can be analyzed with the social and cultural texture analysis identified by Robbins. Social and cultural texture is one of the five textures analyzed using Robbins' Socio-Rhetorical Interpretation model. According to Robbins (Robbins, 1996, p. 71):

> Analysis of the social and cultural texture of a text takes interpreters into sociological and anthropological theory. The issue is not simply the intertexture of a text, but its social and cultural nature as a text. Specific social topics in the text reveal the religious responses to the world in its discourse. Common social and cultural topics in the text exhibit the overall perception of the context in which people live in the world.

The use of the social and cultural texture analyses on these Scriptures identifies the Gnostic-Manipulationist response which seeks a transformed set of relationships or a transformed method of coping with evil. Whereas other orientations reject the goals of society as well as the institutionalized means of attaining them and the existing facilities by which people might be saved, the Gnostic-Manipulationist rejects only the means and the facilities (Robbins, 1996, p. 73). Salvation is possible in the world and evil may be overcome when people learn the right means and improved techniques to deal with their problems. This can be accomplished when people are in one accord.

A Utopian response can also be identified from these Scriptures. The Utopian response seeks to reconstruct the entire social world according to divine given principles, rather than simply to amend it from a reformist position; the goal of a utopian response is to establish a new social organization that will eliminate evil (Robbins, 1996, p. 74). It is much more radical than the reformist response because it insists on complete replacement of the present social organization and differs from the revolutionist response by insisting that people themselves remake the world rather than that a divine power destroy the present world and re-creates another (Robbins, 1996, p. 74). This new social organization called the church will work to remove evil through the concepts of unity and harmony.

Perhaps the strongest response from these Scriptures is the conversionist response which is characterized by a view that the world is corrupt because people are corrupt, and, if people can be changed, the world will be changed (Robbins, 1996, p. 72). Salvation is considered to be available not through objective agencies but only by a profound and supernaturally wrought transformation of the self; the world itself will not change, but the presence of a new subjective orientation to it will itself be salvation (Robbins, 1996, p. 72).

Unity and Harmony: The Total Transformation of Self

This level of conversion and transformation is only available through the power of the Holy Spirit. The unity and harmony that the early church manifested could only come about through a total transformation of the self. This type of organizational structure empowered the early church to flourish in an increasingly hostile environment. The strength of *homothumadon* is in being unanimous, having mutual consent, being in agreement, having group unity, and having one mind or purpose (Mills, 1991).

The Jewish people had been living outside the land of Israel since residents from the northern kingdom of Israel were taken as exiles by Assyria and those from the southern kingdom of Judah were exiled by Babylon. During the Hellenistic era, these Jews of the Diaspora were scattered throughout the Roman Empire and beyond. The long list of place-names mentioned in Acts 2:9-11 is consistent with the literary and inscriptional evidence on the widespread geographic distribution of the Jewish people at this time (Archaeological Study Bible NIV, 2005, p. 1769). After Alexander the Great conquered the eastern lands, the Hellenists and the Hasidim became distinct groups during the period of Greek culture; the Hellenists were succeeded by the Sadducees and the Pharisees considered themselves a direct line from the Hasidim (Gower, 1987, pp. 254-256). However, when Jesus appears on the scene, the very scholars that are supposed to be the most knowledgeable in the land, do not recognize Him and have no interest in His transforming power in their lives. Yet, the people of Israel had a different response.

Diaspora and the Synagogues

While the Diaspora represented the scattered Jewish people outside of Jerusalem, the synagogues were usually the unifying location for those Jews and had four essential functions during Jesus' time (Elwell & Yarbrough, 1998, p. 56):

- It was a school where children were taught the law and Jewish religious traditions.
- It was also a place of worship, where there was recitation of creeds, reading of Scripture, homily, or exposition of Scripture and prayers.
- It functioned as a court where religious or civil questions were settled by the local council.
- It was a place of social interaction, where funerals and special meetings took place and even politics were discussed.

The Diaspora was embedded into the Second Temple period. Paul is faced with the tremendous challenge of changing an entire cultural mindset in establishing the church during this Second Temple Period. The Second Temple Period is commonly understood to be the period of time that the second temple existed from its rebuilding around 530 BC to its destruction by the Romans in 70 AD (Sanders J. T., 2001). Wright contends that during this 600 years of history the Jewish people began looking for the return of a King that would bring peace to the land of Israel which had survived the Babylonian captivity and the rule of the Persians, Greeks, Syrians and finally the Romans (Wright, 1998).

In the strategic plan of God the seeds had been sown for a new king and the Jewish people were looking for their king to return at any moment. Paul was not only dealing with this influence but he was also faced with bringing the Gentiles into the Christian faith. According to DeSilva, the first-century Christians were a minority culture without political power and subject to hostile actions on every hand (DeSilva, 2004, p. 280). Unlike the Essene community of the day, the early church was looking to add new members daily. The Essene community lived outside of Jerusalem in the desert area of the Qumram Valley where the Dead Sea Scrolls have been found. John the Baptist is generally considered to have been a member of the Essene community due to his description and characteristics identified in the Bible. From the social and cultural texture analysis, Robbins would call the Essenes introversionists who viewed the world as evil and withdrew from it (Robbins, 1996, p. 73). While most Essenes prefer to stay isolated from the world, the early church had a greater role to play. Wright concludes that the early church is preparing the people for a new kingdom and a new kingdom message (Wright, 1999).

The synagogue had been the unifying factor for the Diaspora Jews and the early Christians wanted to replace that place of unity with the church. This type of response would be called by Robbins the challenge-response where the challenge is the claim of the early church to replace the social space of the synagogue (Robbins, 1996, p. 80). Robbins would consider the early church as a counterculture or opposite culture rhetoric which rejects the explicit and mutable characteristics of the dominant culture and evokes a new future (Robbins, 1996). This new future would be based on unity and harmony.

Harmony and Strength Based Leadership

Modern organizations can use the successful model of the early church for their development and expansion programs. To move an organization forward, especially during hard times, requires the implementation of the one accord concept. Unity and harmony of thought and purpose is a powerful enabler for organizational growth. Harmony is one of the 34 common talents in the Strength Based Leadership approach to management. For organizations to benefit from the concept of harmony, they need to look for areas of agreement and find that common ground to build upon. Rath provides four main ideas for action to build upon the strength of harmony (Rath, 2007, pp. 110-111):

- Use Harmony talents to build a network of people with differing perspectives. Rely on these people when their expertise is needed.
- When conflict is inevitable, look for points of agreement and engage others in the conversation. By increasing the number of voices in the conversation, points of agreement are more likely to emerge.

- Create interactions and forums in which people feel like their opinions are truly being heard. This will help others become more engaged in group projects and activities.
- In discussions, look for the practical side of things. Help others see this practical side. It is the starting point of agreement.

Unity and harmony become the products of a trusted environment. This level of trust extended the ministry of one man, Jesus, and His 12 disciples to a current worldwide organization of over a billion people. Few, if any, organizations can claim to still be around after 2000 years like the church. None can claim to be as successful. Modern organizations can learn from the early church principles of trust to produce unity and harmony to extend and grow their organizations. Implementing the ideas for action of the Strength Based Leadership theme of harmony would allow modern organizations to build upon the foundation of harmony and produce effective growth. Trust, unity, and harmony worked for the early church, and they will still work for organizations today.

Chapter 8
The Common Core of Ethics

"Educating the mind without educating the heart is
no education at all."
—Aristotle

"Education without values, as useful as it is,
seems rather to make man a more clever devil."
—C.S. Lewis

"Relativity applies to physics, not ethics."
—Thomas Jefferson

Ethics seems to be one of those words that most people think they know but have trouble defining. If individuals have trouble defining ethics, then that concept is only compounded when applied to organizations. If you ask 10 different people the definition of ethics, you will probably get 10 different answers. What if the organization has 100 people or a 1000? Then that organization may have 100 or 1000 different definitions. May states that if ethics were easy and straightforward in our organizations, there would be no need for the plethora of books and articles on the subject; ethical decision making and practice are fraught with difficulties and challenges (May, 2012).

The connection between ethics and leadership as presented by Burns establishes genuine leadership as a morally charged concept that systematically refuses to include, for example, Hitler and other despots on its list of leaders (Burns, 1978). When talking about ethics in organizations, there are two ways of approaching the subject which are the individualistic approach and the communal approach. More often than not, discussions about ethics in organizations reflect only the individualistic approach to moral responsibility and according to this approach, every person in an organization is morally responsible for his or her own behavior, which means that any efforts to change that behavior should focus on the individual (Brown, 1989).

Wren and Bedeian state that the subject of ethics deals with human moral behavior, good or bad, and has occupied the thinking of researchers from the beginning of time (Wren & Bedeian, 2009). According to Ciulla, the study of ethics generally consists of the examination of right, wrong, good, evil, virtue, duty, obligation, rights, justice, fairness, etc. in human relationships with each other and other living things (Ciulla, 2004). When dealing with organizations, an innovative leader can use the three types of leadership values regarding ethics identified by Burns (Ciulla, 2004):

- Ethical virtues—old fashioned character tests such as sobriety, chastity, abstention, kindness, altruism, and other "Ten Commandments" rules of personal conduct.
- Ethical values—honesty, integrity, trustworthiness, reliability, reciprocity, and accountability.
- Moral value—order (or security), liberty, equality, justice, and community (meaning brotherhood and sister-hood, replacing the traditional term fraternity).

When a breakdown in one of these three categories has been noted, a determination of whether the breakdown was individual or communal would benefit the leader in working with the organization to determine the type of ethical breakdown and then develop a plan to restore ethical order.

True Character is Exposed When the Pressure is On

However, as noted above, different people have different definitions of ethics and values. In his foreword to Joanne Ciulla's book ***Ethics, the Heart of Leadership***, James Burns writes (Ciulla, 2004):

> Wouldn't it be lovely, in this fragmented world, if all the sets of values, and hence all the forms of leadership, could exist in happy harmony? Alas, it cannot be. The more that a community embraces ethical virtues of mutual helpfulness, the more it is likely to come into conflict with the ethical virtues of other communities. Ethical values tend to be culture-based and hence diverse. One society's honesty is another society's incivility; one society's reciprocity is another society's corruption.

Again, the complexity of the role of ethics is revealed. Like people, an organization's true character is exposed when the pressure is on. Abraham Lincoln once said that nearly all men can stand adversity, but if you want to test a man's character then give him power. The same can be said about organizations as well as people. Today, many leaders and organizations are rising to the ethical challenge.

World's Most Ethical Companies

The research-based Ethisphere® Institute is a leading international think-tank dedicated to the creation, advancement and sharing of best practices in business ethics, corporate social responsibility, anti-corruption and sustainability. *Ethisphere Magazine*, which publishes the globally recognized World's Most Ethical Companies Ranking™, is the quarterly publication of the Institute. For the 2012 year, a record 145 companies made the Ethisphere World's Most Ethical Companies (WME) list, which included more than three dozen industries, from aerospace to wind power, with 43 of the WME winners headquartered outside the U.S. Since the list's inception, 23 companies have made the list all six years including: Aflac, American Express, Fluor, General Electric, Milliken & Company, Patagonia, Rabobank, and Starbucks, among others.

According to the Ethisphere Institute, the World's Most Ethical Companies designation recognizes companies that truly go beyond making statements about doing business "ethically" and translate those words into action. WME honorees demonstrate real and sustained ethical leadership within their industries, putting into real business practice the Institute's credo of "Good. Smart. Business. Profit." To that end the Institute has developed a 36-page survey to determine an organization's Ethics Quotient (EQTM). While the rating system and analysis is proprietary, the survey is available online and provides a good starting point for today's organizations to develop an ethical framework. The EQTM framework consists of five core categories:

- Ethics and Compliance Program
- Reputation, Leadership and Innovation
- Governance
- Corporate Citizenship and Responsibility
- Culture of Ethics

Large organizations such as the Walt Disney Company and Microsoft have established a Director of Corporate Citizenship to operate the organization in an economically, socially, and environmentally sustainable manner, and to be transparent and accountable for their actions, behaviors, and products. While smaller organizations may not have the resources to create this type of position, the tenets of transparency and accountability can be woven throughout an organization of any size. The establishment of these tenets early in the organization will help ensure their continuity as the organization grows. This type of ethical framework goes beyond simply legal compliance and establishes a culture of ethics and a corporate citizenship responsibility requiring organizations to be responsible not just for their behavior but for their product as well.

Everyone Loves a Good Success Story

Ethical failures seem to be a common front page news story. While is there is some value in understanding the reasons for ethical failures another way of examining the role of ethics in modern organizations is to focus on ethical success stories. While it is important for organizations to know what "not to do," ethical success stories provide a measure for organizations to strive towards. Yet, success stories do not seem to make the headline news story of the day. However, constantly emphasizing ethical failures only leads to a critical or cynical outlook. Many people and organizations make good ethical decisions every day. While some in our modern day society believe that what goes on in private does not affect the outward or public image of today leaders, the current scandals of ethical failures are proving them wrong.

The University of Virginia's Darden School of Business reports in the Business Roundtable Institute for Corporate Ethics that most people know the story of Johnson and Johnson's former CEO Jim Burke and the Tylenol product recall in the 1980s in which, at a great short-term financial cost, he pulled all potentially tampered-with products off the shelves, thereby keeping the public's trust intact. As the story goes, some Tylenol had been laced with cyanide. Three people died in Chicago and seven people died altogether. Tylenol represented 18% of Johnson and Johnson's corporate income and the recall lost the corporation over 100 million dollars. According to the Business Roundtable Institute, the recall and rapid response put Johnson and Johnson in the ethics hall of fame. Many corporations have determined to focus on a successful ethic culture. However, success stories are not just limited to CEO's of Fortune 500 companies.

Ethics that Affects Millions

The works of Professor Mohammed Yunus, a Nobel Prize winner and founder of Grameen Bank as well as being known as the "father" of rural finance in Bangladesh, demonstrate how rural people and the poor can be supported to sustainably pursue their livelihood's development. Through rural finance, Bangladesh is currently a shining example in Asia where microfinance has turned the lives of hundreds of thousands and possibly millions of impoverished individuals and families from a situation of abject poverty and hopelessness to one of dignity and integrity. Former President George W. Bush stated in a speech in New York that, "America's highest economic need is higher ethical standards—enforced by strict laws and upheld by responsible business leaders."

Early Church Leadership

While modern management and leadership literature abounds with theories on how best to achieve ethical efficiency in churches and church related organizations, it is vital to remember the original guiding principles laid down in the Bible through the Apostle Paul's writing to the young minister, Titus. Even though these truths were written almost 2000 years ago, they have withstood the test of time and are still applicable today. According to Low, many managers today are awash with complicated modern management concepts, so much so that the simple, but yet time-tested wisdom enunciated in the Holy Bible is conveniently brushed aside or overlooked (Low, 1999).

Much like today, the early church came under the influence of worldly leaders in the churches once Paul would leave the area to plant other churches. Many of these early churches were small house-groups, led by people who had heard the gospel (Elwell & Yarbrough, 1998, p. 340). However, over time, that leadership often changed hands, and was taken over by people who were unsaved and did not know the gospel. They would take the individual groups into various theological directions, usually of their own background and choosing; this pattern of drifting is evident throughout the development of the early church (Hayford, 1995, p. 421). Consequently, any modern congregation that wishes to be like the "first-century church" should do some historical research before making such a claim. Every group was different, dealt with a myriad of problems, and was struggling to maintain the integrity of the gospel against a world view that was quite contrary to the teachings of Jesus. It was in this setting in Crete that Titus was sent by the Apostle Paul.

Titus in Crete

While Crete is about 170 miles south of the Greek mainland, it is the largest of the Greek islands at 156 miles long and at most 35 miles wide. It was home to the to the Minoan civilization, a Mediterranean culture that reached its high point around 1500 BC but collapsed at the end of the Bronze Age around 1200 BC (Archaeological Study Bible NIV, 2005). Crete is referred to in the Old Testament as Caphtor (Deuteronomy 2:23 and Jeremiah 47:4) and the Philistines came to Canaan by way of Crete (Amos 9:7).

With this backdrop, the Apostle Paul writes a letter to Titus. While Titus is never mentioned in Acts, the references to him in Paul's epistles (13 times) make it clear that he was one of Paul's closest and most trusted fellow-workers in the gospel. When Paul left Antioch for Jerusalem to discuss the gospel (Acts 15:1b) with the leaders there, he took Titus (a Gentile) with him (Gal 2:1-3) as an example of one accepted by grace without circumcision. This fact was used to vindicate Paul's stand on this issue (Gal 2:3-5). It also appears Titus worked with Paul at Ephesus during the third missionary journey. From there the apostle sent him to Corinth where he helped that church with its work and with the collection for the poor saints in Jerusalem (see 2 Cor. 2:12-13; 7:5-6; 8:6).

Early Church Leader Qualifications

Titus 1:5 states that Paul left Titus in Crete to set things in order by appointing leaders in every city that had churches. As Titus attempts to establish the teachings of Jesus and Paul to the churches in the region, he needed some credibility with the people, and some sound advice from Paul is directed both to him and to the congregations. Similar to Paul's letter to Timothy in Ephesus, he writes to Titus in Crete and identifies 14 value and ethical qualifications for early church leaders (HCSB, 2010):

1. One who is blameless
2. The husband of one wife
3. Having faithful children not accused of wildness or rebellion
4. Not arrogant
5. Not hot-tempered
6. Not addicted to wine
7. Not a bully
8. Not greedy for money
9. Hospitable
10. Loving what is good
11. Sensible
12. Righteous
13. Holy
14. Self-controlled

Social and Cultural Texture

Titus chapter 1 can be analyzed with the social and cultural texture analysis identified by Robbins. As previously identified, the social and cultural texture is one of the five textures analyzed using Robbins' Socio-Rhetorical Interpretation model. The social and cultural texture of a given text concerns the nature of the text as a part of a society and culture. This texture emerges from insight into how the text views the world through specific social topics; how it shares cultural attitudes and norms through common social and cultural topics; and how it reveals the dominant cultural system (Robbins, 1996, p. 71). Analysis of Titus ascertains a conversionist response. This response can be found in Titus 1:9-11 (HCSB, 2010).

> Holding to the faithful message as taught, so that he will be able both to encourage with sound teaching and to refute those who contradict it. For there are also many rebellious people, full of empty talk and deception, especially those from Judaism. It is necessary to silence them; they overthrow whole households by teaching what they shouldn't in order to get money dishonestly.

Verse 9 also reveals that the purpose of early church leadership is to function as a gatekeeper of the teachings of Jesus through Paul. Additional text analysis also discovers a Gnostic-Manipulationist response. The Gnostic-Manipulationist response seeks a transformed set of relationships or a transformed method of coping with evil. Whereas other orientations reject the goals of society as well as the institutionalized means of attaining them and the existing facilities by which people might be saved, the Gnostic-Manipulationist rejects only the means and the facilities (Robbins, 1996). Salvation is possible in the world and evil may be overcome when people learn the right means and improved techniques to deal with their problems.

Paul has left Titus in Crete in order to overcome the false teachings that have spread throughout the churches. Verses 10 and 11 also support the Gnostic-Manipulationist response by identifying that many rebellious people are working against the gospel of the Kingdom. Additionally, a Cretan poet also labeled his fellow Cretans as liars and lazy gluttons in verse 12. Although the original text is no longer available, this is supposed to have been written by Epimenides who was a sixth century BC native of Crete held in high esteem by the Cretans (Archaeological Study Bible NIV, 2005).

A utopian response is also evident. The utopian response seeks to reconstruct the entire social world according to divine given principles, rather than simply to amend it from a reformist position; the goal of a utopian response is to establish a new social organization that will eliminate evil (Robbins, 1996). It is much more radical than the reformist response because it insists on complete replacement of the present social organization and differs from the revolutionist response by insisting that people themselves remake the world rather than that a divine power destroy the present world and re-creates another (Robbins, 1996). From this response, Titus is identified as the gatekeeper to reconstruct and set back in order the churches in Crete.

The Gatekeeper Role

Paul instructs Titus to use "sound teaching" in order to bring about a change in the Cretans and to refute the false teachings. As the early Christian church grew, it experienced many challenges brought on by its vision and its growth (DeSilva, 2004). Paul's letter is designed to provide Titus with some valuable knowledge and experience in dealing with these challenges. Titus and the letters to Timothy are collectively referred to as Paul's Pastoral Epistles because they are written to individuals entrusted with the oversight of specific congregations; they directly concern the role and responsibilities of the leader (DeSilva, 2004, p. 732).

According to this text, the primary role of Christian leaders is sound teaching. They are to instruct others in godly living regardless of their station in life and to guard God's church from false teachers and deceivers attempting to take advantage of the people of God (Hayford, 1995). The godly leaders' teaching is to be first through their life and people should be able to look at the Christian leader and say that is how I am supposed to live. Paul is instructing Titus in how to control the flow of the truth of the gospel and how to refute the false teachings. In other words, Paul wants Titus to become a gatekeeper for the gospel message.

The business definition of gatekeeper is a junior officer who controls the flow of information to a group of people (BusinessDictionary.com, 2012). German researchers, Hauschildt and Schewe, conclude that in order to be successful, new organizations must establish the role of the gatekeeper who is charged with maintaining the original purpose and content of information so that it does not drift (again) or change over time (Hauschildt & Schewe, 2000). With this new organization called the Christian church, Paul is setting up Titus to be the protector and gatekeeper of the sound doctrine for the island of Crete. According to tradition, Paul also ordained Titus as Archbishop of Crete, and he died there in 107 AD around the age of 95 (Catholic Encyclopedia, 2009).

Titus as Gatekeeper

The essence of ethics is to keep things in order. As the gatekeeper, Titus was to set in order the things that were lacking as instructed in Titus 1:5. The Greek word "to set in order" is epidiorthoo (Strong, 1981). According to the Englishman's Greek Concordance, the Greek word *epidiorthoo* is only used one time in the entire New Testament, which is Titus 1:5 (Wigram, 1979, p. 283). Thayer simply defined *epidiorthoo* as setting in order besides or further what still remains to be set in order (Thayer, 1983, p. 238). However, Vine contends that *epidiorthoo* is used in the sense of setting right again what was defective, not to add to what the Apostle Paul had done, but to restore what had fallen into disorder since Paul had left Crete; this is suggested by the prefix *epi* (Vine, 1985, p. 827). The role and definition of the gatekeeper would support either definition, but would better identify with Vines by setting up a person to restore and set in order the original purpose and content of information so that it does not drift (again) or change over time. Paul is placing a tremendous amount of faith and trust in a former Gentile of the Greek persuasion to be the gatekeeper and instructor of sound doctrine to the Cretans. Only a highly trusted and valued co-worker could be placed in this influential ethical position.

Modern Day Application

Modern day organizations face similar challenges that Titus faced. According to Blackaby, part of the challenge with Christian leadership is that many of the Christian leaders are taught the same thing as secular leaders, and the current generation of Christian leaders is immersed in the popular secular leadership writings of the day (Blackaby & Blackaby, 2001, p. 9). As organizational values become aligned to popular secular values, Christian based values and ethics may become set aside. For example, are churches focusing on the Great Commission or writing mission statements? While there is nothing wrong with mission statements, it should not be the focus of the church. Values and value alignment are based in the worldview of the current leader and many Christian leaders are trained in secular organizations with a secular worldview. Noebel concludes that the tug-of-war between and among worldviews that currently rages in America and around the world divide those who hold traditional Christian ideas and values from those who hold various liberal/radical Humanist views (Noebel, 2006, p. 19). Gangel identifies that there is a growing encroachment of secular leaders bringing their secular styles of leadership into the church and add a Scripture verse to it in order to call it Christian (Gangel, 1981, p. 25).

The biblical values and ethics presented above suggest that modern day mangers and leaders should, likewise, be blameless; spiritually stable or balanced (not an extremist); sober-minded and able to prioritize; respectable and hospitable; able to communicate truths; have self-control and is not addicted to drinking, gambling, etc.; not self-centered or takes advantage of people; not quick-tempered, temperamental or moody; not physically aggressive; gentle and not abusive in words; not materialistic; cares for his subordinates; loves what is good and devoted to holy living; just and fair; and does not politicize or use another person as his "mouthpiece" or generate ill feelings among people (Lee, 1997).

Walt Disney and the Gatekeeper Role

The Walt Disney Company faced an ethical dilemma that the gatekeeper concept helped resolve. After the death of Walt Disney, the leadership of the Walt Disney Company developed a program called "Traditions" to impart the importance of Disney ethics, culture, heritage, values and policies as originally taught by Walt Disney (Disney Institute, 2001, p. 45). With the Traditions class firmly in place and currently taught to every employee (called cast members) on their first day at work, the visionary process of Walt Disney was restored and kept in order. The Walt Disney Company was concerned that without Walt Disney leading the company its original purpose and content of information would drift or change over time. The Traditions course provides for the role of the gatekeeper for the entire Walt Disney Company, and still promotes the Disney brand of ethics to all its cast members.

The Ethics Gatekeeper

Modern day churches and organizations would benefit from following the instruction in Titus and the example of the Walt Disney Company in establishing a gatekeeper role or program to keep the organization on its original course and purpose. Organizational drift quickly occurred in the churches of Crete. However, Paul responded just as quick with a solution of establishing Titus as a gatekeeper of sound doctrine as well as identifying 14 value and ethical requirements for leaders that allowed him to continue moving the ministry forward without having to backtrack and take care of problems that were occurring over time.

The Walt Disney Company instituted a gatekeeper program that allowed them to grow even larger that when Walt Disney was at the helm and allowed them to retain much of his original purpose and intent. Modern day churches and organizations would greatly benefit by establishing the role of the gatekeeper as well as having the 14 value and ethical qualifications from Titus built into their modern leadership development programs and replace the secular aggressive-based value and ethical programs.

Ethical Considerations

As emerging innovative leaders of today's modern organizations, it is vital to be able to develop and acknowledge ethical success stories as well as having knowledge of ethical failures. Many business and leaders around the world are making successful ethical decisions on a daily basis. Two keys to building a successful ethical organization are to establish a culture of ethics through the gatekeeper role and a corporate citizenship responsibility inside the organization. Many organizations have developed a Director of Corporate Citizenship position to transform organizational cultures to extend beyond just behavior, but to also include their products. With many small organizations being able to access the global business economy through the use of the Internet, the ethical tenets of transparency and accountability are becoming even more important. The common core of ethics may be the most complex, yet the most required core, for innovative leaders.

Chapter 9
The Common Core of Context

"Reality is not a function of the event as an event,
but of the relationship of that event to past, and future, events."
—Robert Penn Warren, All the King's Men

"Priority is a function of context."
—Stephen R. Covey

"Nothing worth doing is completed in our lifetime; therefore we must be saved by hope. Nothing true or beautiful makes complete sense in any immediate context of history; therefore we must be saved by faith. Nothing we do, however virtuous, can be accomplished alone; therefore, we are saved by love."
—Reinhold Niebuhr (American theologian, 1892-1971).

Context is vital for all levels of communication and context is one of the major considerations for innovative leaders to communicate cross-culturally, which makes this common core of special interest to innovative leaders. Whether the subject is an exegetical analysis of Scripture or a new organizational policy, context is a key ingredient. Many times information taken out-of-context will become problematic. Context in a cross-cultural environment is even more critical. According to Morden, it is unrealistic to take an ethnocentric and universalistic view towards the principles and practice of management as they are applied in other countries and other cultures because what works well in one country may be entirely inappropriate in another (Morden, 1999). Again, Shahin and Wright conclude that most leadership theories come from North America and may not be applicable across diverse cultures and ethnic groups, which differ from the American culture (Shahin & Wright, 2004). Morden further states that context is defined in terms of how individuals and their society seek information and knowledge (Morden, 1999). Von Krough et al. contend that the ability to create the right context is the enabling context for knowledge creation, and involves organizational structures that foster solid relationships and effective collaboration (Von Krogh, Ichijo, & Nonaka, 2000, p. 176).

Hofstede identifies that mental programs are developed early in childhood and are reinforced in schools and organizations, which leads to the development of a national culture; consequently, these values are expressed differently among people from different countries (Hofstede, 1984, p. 11). Hall distinguishes between a high-context culture and a low-context culture. People from high-context cultures obtain information from personal information networks; whereas, people from low-context cultures seek information about decisions and deals from a research base (Hall, 1976). A high-context culture places a great deal of emphasis on a person's values and position or place in society, and interactions with others, rather than on the words and formal legalistic constructs (Darling & Heller, 2011). The identification and use of cultural context takes time, experience, and practice. There are no quick solutions for understanding the context of a culture.

The Context Strategy

With the advent of globalization and with cultural interaction becoming more prevalent, developing a cross-cultural communication context strategy takes on an added dimension. However, Northouse determines that there are no established theories of cultural leadership so research becomes more of a collection of related ideas instead of a single unified theory (Northouse, 2007, p. 301). Finzel identifies communication chaos as one of the top ten mistakes that leaders make and conclude that communication strategies must have cross-cultural considerations in order to reduce chaos (Finzel, 1994, p. 113). As previously mentioned, trust becomes the outcome of effective communication across different cultures. According to Sendjaya and Pekerti, trust is a mutual benefit derived from effective cross-cultural relationships (Sendjaya & Pekerti, 2010). The establishment of relationships is a critical component of a context strategy.

However, Hofstede remarks that highlighting culture dependent differences in thinking and acting are not always welcome interventions (Hofstede, 1984, p. 8). Hall introduces the concept of context as a human behavioral influence, and he characterizes societies as being either low-context, which are typical of northern Europe, or high-context, most dramatically represented by Japan (Hall E., 1976). Context even affects language, and human speech patterns will change, depending upon who they are speaking to and the context of the communication. Marquardt and Berger settle that one of the problems of the twenty-first century workplace will involve mergers across disparate cultures, and organizations will need to respond in different ways depending on the cultural needs (Marquardt & Berger, 2000, pp. 175-176). The context of those cultural needs will necessitate the different responses.

High-Low Context

Hall states that one of the functions of culture is to provide a selective screen between man and the outside world, which designates what we choose to see as well as ignore (Hall E., 1976, p. 85). Hofstede explains that organizations are culture bound (Hofstede, 1984, p. 252). Morden determines that context is defined in terms of how individuals and their society seek information and knowledge (Morden, 1999). Again, this range of context goes from low to high. According to Schein, low-context events have universal meanings and high context events have various meanings, which can become problematic in different cultures (Schein, 1997, p. 100). People from high context cultures obtain information from personal information networks (Morden, 1999).

Before high context people make a decision, or arrange a deal, they become well informed about the facts associated with it. High context people have discussed the matter with friends, business acquaintances, and relatives as well as asking questions and listening to gossip (Morden, 1999). Hall further recognizes that messages are placed on a continuum between high-context and low context with high context having very little in the coded, explicit, transmitted part of the message; a low context message is just the opposite with the mass of the information being vested in the explicit code (Hall E., 1976, p. 91). Bass summarizes the difference between high-low context cultures when Japan, a high context culture, places a premium on listening as well as the value of agreement with criticism being more indirect through a peer because direct criticism from a leader would cause them to lose face or honor (Bass B., 2008, p. 1037).

Context and Change

According to Kotter, many organizations have a leadership deficit because the organization ignores the leadership potential in the members of that organization, thereby, not offering training or relevant role models to raise up leaders from within (Kotter, 2005). Kotter further contends that great leaders get others to move in a direction that is sensible for themselves, the business, and community (Kotter, 2005). Deming outlined three steps to get others involved in accomplishing transformative change (Deming, 1994):

- The transformative leader has a theory and understands why the transformation would bring gains to the organization as well as the people involved in the organization.
- The transformative leader feels compelled to accomplish the transformation as an obligation to the people and the organization.
- The transformative leader has a step-by-step plan and can explain it in simple terms.

For leaders to be successful in getting other cultures involved in the change process, the leader needs to convey the true meaning behind the need to change. The understanding of this meaning can help alleviate some resistance to change. According to Ulrich and Ulrich, meaning is the object of a nearly universal search, and work is a nearly universal setting for engaging in this quest; therefore, leaders are meaning makers (Ulrich & Ulrich, 2010):

- They set direction that inspires others.
- They help others participate in doing good work.

- They communicate ideas and invest in practices that shape how people think, act, and feel.

As leaders focus on getting others involved in the change process and conveying the change in clear and simple terms, resistance should decrease and readiness should increase. This process is also part of the continuous improvement process for understanding other cultures.

Innovators never stop learning, which produces a continuous improvement mindset related to change. According to Locke and Jain, the concept of continuous improvement has attracted a great deal of research and managerial interest in recent years (Locke & Jain, 1995). Covey concludes that the most powerful investment that people can ever make in their lives is their investment in continuous learning and continuous improvement (Covey, 1989, p. 289). The adoption of a continuous learning process is a vital component of a leader's growth and global leadership development. Buckler identifies that three ingredients are needed for the continuous learning process to be effective (Buckler, 1996):

- Focus to plot a course for the learning effort.
- An environment which facilitates learning.
- Techniques which enable learning to be efficient.

Context and Authenticity

Context helps knowledge and information become authentic. Authenticity can lead to the development of an authentic leadership model. According to Bennis, leadership without perspective, which leads to a point of view, is not leadership and a person cannot borrow a point of view any more than a person can borrow someone else's eyes; leadership must be authentic and original because each person is an original (Bennis W. G., 1992). From their work in Israel in 2005, Shamir and Eilam identify a four-component framework for defining authentic leadership, which includes that authentic leaders (Shamir & Eilam, 2005):

- Do not fake their leadership.
- Do not lead for status, honor, or other personal rewards.

- Are not copies but are originals.
- Are leaders whose actions are based on values and convictions.

A global leader developing a cross-cultural communication strategy should be an original and follow the framework of an authentic leader. Noted author John Mason claims that everyone is born an original and should not die a copy (Mason, 1993). In identifying what a 21st century global leader should look like, George states that today's leaders should be authentic, unique, and the genuine article as well as concluding that the only valid test of a leader is the ability to bring people together to achieve sustainable results over time (George, 2007). Applying George's conclusion to measure today's leaders may help discover who are acting and who are being authentic especially in a cross cultural environment.

Cross Cultural Context

Misapplied context in a cross cultural environment can produce a malfunctioning organizational culture. According to Fletcher and Jones, a malfunctioning organizational culture will be reflected in such indicators as poor quality of work, low levels of commitment to the organization, individuals working below capacity, high levels of absenteeism, labor turnover, poor health, alcoholism, stress, and a poor safety record (Fletcher & Jones, 1992). Madu and Jacob argue that the internet will lead to a global cross cultural transformation that will enhance global business operations by removing cultural barriers that lead to sub-optimal business operations (Madu & Jacob, 1991).

With the advent of the Internet and the global economy within many organizational frameworks, cross-cultural considerations become paramount. Many times, what is normal and acceptable in one culture is an insult in another culture. In addition to wisdom, research and communication become key aspects of building trust relationships. However, it is important to keep in mind that individuals interact with individuals, not cultures (Morrison & Conaway, 2006). According to Northouse, determining the basic dimensions and characteristics of cultures are the first step in understanding these relationships (Northouse, 2007).

Canton contends that sustainable globalization will increase cross-cultural understanding by breaking down barriers among people of different nations as trade alliances grow across borders (Canton, 2006). As these barriers are removed, new communication strategies will arise.

Context and Communication Strategies

Innovators need to discover a communication strategy that is congruent to the survival of the organization by understanding the cultural context of the people. Research at the Bucharest Academy of Economic Studies states that a communication strategy is vital to the success of modern day organizations (Rodica, 2009). LaChance concludes that it's nearly impossible for an organization to perform in concert at a very high level unless all the employees are responding to a common communication strategy (LaChance, 2006). According to Kaplan and Norton an effective strategic learning process requires a shared strategic framework that communicates the strategy and enables all participants, regardless of culture, to see how their individual activities contribute to overall strategy fulfillment (Kaplan & Norton, 2001).

The Mälardalen University School of Business in Västerås, Sweden ascertains three features of developing a communication strategy to assist organizations (Johanson, Skoog, Backlund, & Almqvist, 2006):

- First, the features of connectivity, regularity and stability have the potential to assist more comprehensively in allocating attention to, and control of, the organization in relation to the defined management control and communication strategy.
- Second, these features may also enable managers to balance their attention to those items on the agenda that must be dealt with strictly on time, to meet certain operational goals.
- Third, if certain relations and connections over time are clarified, their features may assist managers in communicating and legitimizing certain activities that would be harder to legitimize, given data that are more ad hoc or structured in completely different ways.

Context in Structured and Unstructured Environments

The work by Hofstede recognizes the degree to which people prefer structure over unstructured situations. Adding to Hofstede, the second dimension of national culture has been labeled the Uncertainty Avoidance, which identifies that uncertainty about the future is a basic fact of human life through which structure is introduced in order to reduce uncertainty (Hofstede, 1984, p. 110). Bass concludes that one striking difference between organizations that differ substantially in size is how relationships become more structured and formalized in large organizations, and the Aston Model was developed to include two major organizational factors (Bass B. , 2008, p. 738):

- The structuring of activities (prescribed work roles).
- The centralization of decision making (limits on distraction).

However, Galbraith cautions that structure is only one facet of organizational design, and structure can become overemphasized when it affects status or power rather than processes, rewards, and people (Galbraith J., 2002, p. 14). While structure is important to the overall direction and focus of the organization, it becomes critical that the organization does not get distracted from taking care of its people. Lee Cockerell, the former Executive Vice President of Operations at the Walt Disney World Resorts, admitted that early in his career he thought a strong brand was the most important thing in an organization. However, he soon realized that the people were the brand, and no matter how good the products or services became, an organization cannot achieve true excellence unless they can attract great people (Cockerell, 2008, pp. 85-86). Finzel concludes that one of the top ten mistakes that leaders make is putting paperwork ahead of "peoplework", and the greater the leadership role, the more important the "peoplework" (Finzel, 1994, p. 37). As emerging innovative leaders develop an understanding of the common core of context, interpersonal relationships will begin to grow and expand thereby increasing their influence and success in the organization.

Chapter 10
The Common Core of Foresight & Forecasting

"The best way to predict the future is to invent it."
—Immanuel Kant

"To expect the unexpected shows a thoroughly modern intellect."
—Oscar Wilde

"It is said that the present is pregnant with the future."
—Voltaire in The Portable Voltaire

"Time Keeps on Slippin' Slippin' Slippin' into the Future."
—Steve Miller Band

A popular song from the 1970's is "Fly Like an Eagle" by the Steve Miller Band. This song went to #2 in January 1977 (Relative, 2008). Steve Miller's orientation of time was to fly into the future for a solution to present day problems. Not a bad idea. However, time orientation is not just reserved for song lyrics. According to Greenberger and Thoms, time orientation is implicit in leadership theory and explicit in leadership practice, which makes it worthy of further study (Greenberger & Thoms, 1995). Burns also identifies that developing time schemes are important in leadership theory and practice (Burns, 1978). Graham proposes that time conception is a set of basic beliefs about life that are established in a cultural context, and he described three patterns of time (Graham, 1981):

- Time as a procedural tradition
- Time as a circular tradition
- Time as a linear separable tradition

Hall determines three concepts to account for cultural differences among people: time, context, and space. He further concludes that tasks can be handled through monochronicity (single tasked) or polychronicity (multi-tasked) (Hall, 1989). Research at the University of Hong Kong concludes that people approach tasks from a monochronic and/or polychronic time orientation based upon their dominant culture of upbringing (Zhang, Goonetilleke, Plocher, & Liang, 2004). Morden notes that national cultures can be derived based upon monochronicity or polychronicity, but the mixing of monochronic and polychronic cultures may give rise to constant culture clash and disagreement (Morden, 1999). As futurists are building scenarios, it is vital to understand the time orientation of the national culture and/or organization in order to view the possible futures.

Forward Thinking

For innovators, change is an ever-present reality. Therefore, the real question is what to do next with these ever-changing environments. This is where the common core of foresight and forecasting become paramount. Bass contends that leaders need to be intuitive about what comes next and try to make it happen (Bass B., 2008, p. 688). Hines concludes that forecasting should be part of the fabric of every organization, and innovative thinking should be internalized into the entire institution because it is mission critical for any organization's future (Hines, 2006).

Can tomorrow really be seen today? The discipline of forecasting boldly declares "yes" to this question. Slaughter defines forecasting simply as forward thinking and claims that it is a mental process that is used every day: such as taking out a raincoat or an umbrella in case of rain; thinking of a convenient time to make an appointment; saving up for something; or taking precautions to avoid something (Slaughter, 1993). Taylor concludes that forecasting is a predication of what may occur in the future through the use of mathematical methods (Taylor III, 1996, p. 581). Hines considers forecasting one of the six elements of an innovative foresight framework and involves uncertainties, tools, diverging and converging approaches, and alternatives (Hines, 2006). According to Cornish, forecasting is used alongside of futuring, futurism, and future studies (Cornish, 2005, p. xi).

However, innovative forecasting is not simply about the future. Slaughter contends that the extent that we become aware of different future alternatives, we gain access to new choices in the present (Slaughter, 1993). In other words, appropriate action in the present can be determined based upon a future scenario. This could involve a scenario to avoid a future event or a scenario to create a future event. It could also be used to decide upon an action due to an impending future event. Corporate and business leaders today can incorporate these future-related scenarios into their daily decision making processes in order to produce one of their futures.

Just as the present day environment is made up of the sum total of past decisions, so the future will become the product of decisions made today. Part of the integrated definition of leadership by Winston and Patterson includes influence by humbly conveying a prophetic vision of the future in clear terms that resonates with the follower(s) beliefs and values in such a way that the follower(s) can understand and interpret the future into present-time action steps (Winston & Patterson, 2006). Successful leaders discover ways to connect their vision to the values of the organization and establish a clear vision to include the values of the followers in the organization. Patterns of activity for organizations begin to emerge as the product of connecting possible future events to current actions for the innovative leader.

Pattern Masters

Peters identifies that a future consciousness depends upon an awareness of the possibility that the future can be different from the present and the past (Peters, 1978, p. 68). This denotes the need for future leaders to be able to identify patterns. Keidel concludes that future effective leaders, managers, and organizations will comprehend their future as they become "pattern masters" being able to resolve conflicts and communicate their vision through innovative processes (Keidel, 1995, p. 139). Successful organizations of today must keep moving forward looking for new competitive advantages and becoming a "pattern master" that can lead the way. As the new leaders begin to empower workers, it is important to understand that people tend to work better cooperatively rather than competitively. According to Deming, the understanding of this profound knowledge will lead to a transformation of management which leads to the adoption of a system, and systems work best when people learn to work cooperatively rather than competitively (Deming, 1994, p. 116).

Taylor concludes that when organizations start forecasting, or predicting what may occur in the future, the most important component of the newly forecasted organization are the people who will build the organization as well as the consumers that the organization will service (Taylor III, 1996, pp. 580-581). Replacing a competitive organizational structure with a more productive cooperative environment is not just a Deming idea for North America. Research in China reveals that productivity and people maintenance values have traditionally been considered to contribute to leadership effectiveness, and cooperative rather than competitive goal interdependence mediates the relationship between these outcomes as well as determining that productivity and people-values coupled with cooperative goals provide a foundation for effective leadership (Liu, Yu, & Tjosvold, 2002). A cooperative framework paves the way for organizations to produce scenario based futures.

Scenario-Based Futures

Scenario planning is the process of developing and using a set of scenarios to explore and test decision options. Chermack notes that it is important to understand that scenarios are not strategies, but are stories of possible future environments and he identifies five phases of performance-based scenario systems (Chermack, 2011, p. 80):

- **Phase 1**- Project Preparation: Intent - Develop the purpose and define the key issue. The important stakeholder groups should be identified, individuals with a high degree of organization knowledge should be recruited, internal leaders at all levels of the organization should be identified, and the scenario team can be assembled. The scenario team manages the project.
- **Phase 2**- Scenario Exploration: Intent - Gather data using SWOT, forecasts, trend analysis, Social, Technological, Economic, Ecological, and Political (STEEP) Analysis, etc. This phase involves data gathering both on a general level and on the specific issue under consideration. The goal of information gathering is to

learn and to expand the project team's familiarity with the industry and relevant economic and social factors. A secondary goal is to gather information relevant to the specific issue or decision articulated in the project proposal. Everyone has biases, and they show up in scenario planning. A key skill is the ability to be aware of biases and head off confinement in thinking.

- **Phase 3**- Scenario Development: Intent – Develop workshops and exercises to build an innovative conversation. In scenario planning, the foundation of internal analysis is the interviews. The interviews conducted allow access to the deepest concerns of line workers, managers, and executives. Interviewing individuals or groups of people in an organization is a time-consuming and detailed process that requires commitment and skill. The next step is aimed at creating the scenario logics. The scenario logics are the general frameworks or the plots of the scenarios. Once the participants have ranked the issues by impact on the strategic agenda, and by uncertainty, the ranking space is divided roughly into a 2 x 2 matrix and named. The scenario titles are critical. Naming scenarios has to do with branding and providing titles that conjure up the concepts of the scenarios will make them memorable. Once the scenario logics have been constructed and the basic plots of four scenarios have been defined, each subgroup should task an individual to write the detailed scenario story.
- **Phase 4**- Scenario Implementation: Intent- Shows how to put the scenarios to use. The first step in putting the scenarios to use is to return to the initial purpose, problem, and question. After all, the priority of the project is to develop a variety of different ways to explore the problem and answer the question. This workshop can be informal and needs only to bring the team and decision-makers back together in a room suitable for brainstorming. The presentations should be short, involve the essence of the stories, and use colorful pictures or presentation slides to describe each scenario. The project leader then facilitates a dialogue relating back to the initial question for each scenario.
- **Phase 5**- Project Assessment: Measuring the actual outcomes relative to the expected outcomes. The goal of scenario planning is to begin a genuine conversation about the potential issues decision-

makers may face, and to provide a mechanism to wonder about the future. Scenarios are not forecasts and the purpose is not to choose a scenario. Scenarios are not strategies. Scenarios provide different contexts in which to consider the risks, benefits, and implications of decisions and different ways of managing strategic options.

Futurists—Not Fortune Tellers

Modern futurism properly cultivates human foresight and ethical choice (Gary, 2008). The secular futurist is trying to look at the future through glasses that only have one lens. Unfortunately for them, this will only produce a future with a fuzzy and grainy image. Christian eschatologists with a Biblical worldview have a distinct advantage over the secular futurists because they get to use the best of both worlds. Not only do they get to take advantage of the work of the secular futurists, but they also get to tap into a divine source to help with the future.

Gary further determines that more dialogue between futurists and religionists could identify conceptual and methodological parallels in forecasting (Gary, 2008). In other words, the two working together could accomplish so much more. According to Peters, the future itself, even in secular circles, seems to take on many of the qualities ordinarily ascribed to the divine: mystery, transcendence, an extra-human power to save the people, and an ability to determine the ultimate value (or non-value) of anything that exists in the present (Peters, 1978, p. 15). However, many secular futurists tend to focus only on earthly powers. Horsley and Silberman stated that early Christianity was, in fact, a down-to-earth response to an oppressive ideology of earthly power that had recently swept across continents, disrupted economies and overturned ancient traditions (Horsley & Silberman, 2002, p. 10). Vision is much better when seen through two lenses: earthly power and divine interaction. This type of cooperative arrangement can lead to the further development of forecasting tools.

Tools

Analysts and organizational leaders can gain valuable insight and experience by having practical knowledge of the variety and uses of forecasting tools. Properly used, these tools can help analysts and leaders gain an advantage in helping organizations meet their current goals as well as building the organization for the future. Hines and Bishop said that there are many different tools or approaches an analyst can choose from for performing innovative foresight, and it is important to choose the tools well-suited to the activity at hand (Hines & Bishop, 2006, p. 98). Scenario planning is an excellent tool to choose when organizations need to look at a variety of potential futures. Chermack recognized that scenario planning is a tool for surfacing assumptions so that changes can be made in how decision makers see the environment, and it is a useful tool for changing as well as improving the quality of people's perception (Chermack, 2011, p. 3).

According to Bell and Tunnicliff, true foresight and futures development is not the product of one or two people at the top, but the product of many people's visions working together (Bell & Tunnicliff, 1996). According to Hughes and Beatty, strategy is a learning process, and effective innovative leader's use thinking, acting and influencing to make strategy a learning process (Hughes & Beatty, 2005). Tools become an effective device to enable a learning process. The UK based Advanced Institute of Management Research identifies that the SWOT (Strengths, Weaknesses, Opportunities and Threats) analysis is easily the most popular tool available, but the tools with the most users are not necessarily the ones considered by managers as the most valuable (Jarzabkowski, Giulietti, & Oliveira, 2011). Isherwood advocates that while the SWOT analysis was the most used tool, the Game Theory was the most known, but least used tool followed by Cultural Web Analysis and Value Chain Analysis; the Innovative Clock was the least known and least used tool which inferred that simpler tools are used more than complicated tools (Isherwood, 2011).

Cornish concludes that for a futures wheel, participants simply write a possible future event with a circle around it, and then expand the map with a series of possible consequences (Cornish, 2005, p. 131). The value that this procedure brings to the arena of forecasting is looking at the potential second and third order effects of decisions. Hines and Bishop report that the traditional method for identifying second and higher order implications is the futures wheel and that many organizations stop their planning at first order implications thereby failing to get potentially important downstream implications (Hines & Bishop, 2006, p. 146). The futures wheel can increase the awareness of the organization's leaders to the possible implications of their decisions. Watson determines that the future will not be a singular experience nor is it a foregone conclusion and people of the same age, with the same job, living on the same street will experience the future in different ways, which will be heavily influenced by local as well as highly personal events (Watson, 2012, p. 296).

These types of "life experiences" are produced by second and third effects to decision points made in the past. From a Biblical Christian point of view, these implications can be aligned with every person having a unique, distinct plan and purpose developed by the Lord as mentioned in Jeremiah 29:11. Hebrews 11:1 states that faith is the substance of things hoped for, the evidence of things not seen (Spirit Filled Life Bible (NKJV), 1991). Hope and faith work together to provide a picture of the future. According to Sanders, visual thinking is the key to innovative thinking, and innovative thinking has two major components: insight about the present and foresight about the future (Sanders T. I., 1998). Innovative leaders that can look into the possible futures of an organization can quickly become invaluable to leading the growth and expansion of that organization.

Chapter 11
The Common Core of Rest & Renewal

"Liturgy is like a strong tree whose beauty is derived from the continuous renewal of its leaves, but whose strength comes from the old trunk, with solid roots in the ground."
—Pope Paul VI (1897-1978)

"Rest is not idleness, and to lie sometimes on the grass under the trees on a summer's day, listening to the murmur of water, or watching the clouds float across the sky, is by no means a waste of time"
—John Lubbock
English Biologist and Politician, 1834-1913

"Every person needs to take one day away. A day in which one consciously separates the past from the future. Jobs, family, employers, and friends can exist one day without any one of us, and if our egos permit us to confess, they could exist eternally in our absence. Each person deserves a day away in which no problems are confronted, no solutions searched for. Each of us needs to withdraw from the cares which will not withdraw from us."
—Maya Angelou, ***Wouldn't Take Nothing for My Journey Now***

"Jesus calls us to His rest, and meekness is His method. The meek man cares not at all who is greater than he, for he has long ago decided that the esteem of the world is not worth the effort."
—A.W. Tozer, ***Pursuit of God***

Rest and renewal are often-forgotten topics of leadership (Vanderpyl, 2012). Today's leaders are pressed on every side to produce more with less, and work until the project is finished. Bass concludes that U.S. employees work longer hours than their European counterparts in order to maintain a higher output of products which is a major cause of stress (Bass B., 2008, p. 813). According to Maslach and Leiter, organizations are enhancing productivity through the use of sophisticated technology to get more done with fewer people (Maslach & Leiter, 1997, p. 5).

The topic of rest was introduced by God in Genesis 2:1-3 (HCSB, 2010):

> So the heavens and the earth and everything in them were completed. By the seventh day God completed His work that He had done, and He rested on the seventh day from all His work that He had done. God blessed the seventh day and declared it holy, for on it He rested from His work of creation.

Obviously, the Creator of the Heavens and the Earth did not need to rest. Yet, rest is mentioned twice in these two verses. Robbins concludes that the sacred texture analysis describes a systemic and creative study of Scripture that provides insights regarding the nature of the relationship between Divine life and human life (Robbins, 1996, p. 120). Shillington indicates that the sacred texture refers to biblical text from a religious community to a religious community, and when complemented with theological interpretation yields valuable results (Shillington, 2002, p. 279). One insight from this text is that God is introducing the principles of rest and renewal. If it is good for the Divine life, then it must be good for the human life.

This time of rest and renewal from Genesis 2:1-3 comes after a time of spiritual activity. As mentioned in chapter one, Cummings determines that creation may represent one of the first acts of the self-emptying service of God, and another in the self-emptying act of the Word becoming flesh in John chapter one (Cummings, 2004). Both creation and incarnation reveal God's presence and action in divine history. The sacred texture analysis of John chapter one reveals how historical events such as creation and the incarnation represent purposeful steps in the coming of the kingdom of

God as well as God's actions behind the scenes of history with a plan already established by God. Rest should be noted as being one of the purposeful actions in these events. Wuellner contends that spiritual responses can cause fatigue (Wuellner, 1998, p. 115). God prescribes rest in Genesis 2:1-3 after completing spiritual activity.

Many times, leaders are revered for their work ethic, but rarely for their "rest ethic" (Vanderpyl, 2012). According to Maslach and Leiter, work overload is a leading cause of burnout, and burnout greatly affects the bottom line of any organization (Maslach & Leiter, 1997, p. 65). Covey contends that success in life involves caring for the physical dimension in getting sufficient rest and relaxation (Covey, 1989, p. 289). O'Neil states that no success is worth the high toll it can take on a person's health, relationships, and peace of mind (O'Neil, 1993, p. 84). Burn out can become the product of this high toll.

Burn Out

Burn out is the likely product of over extending commitments in life. However, cultural influences can provide strength during a time of extended commitments for a short period of time. Nadler and Tushman determine that culture is centered in the ideologies, political alliances, collective self-images, webs of influence, career expectations, and patterns of behavior in people (Nadler & Tushman, 1997, p. 194). Research at the University of the South Pacific in Fiji identify that culture influences our thinking and consequently our behaviors, and social justice is about recognizing our values, philosophies, processes, and structures in our education system and that theorizing social justice should be founded on our knowledge systems that are embedded in our cultures (Fua, 2007). Hofstede defines culture as the programming of the mind that differentiates one group from another group (Hofstede, 2001). According to Bass, cultures clearly differ in what are seen as important traits of character (Bass B., 2008, p. 221). It is these components of culture and family that provides the strengths needed to accomplish individual purpose. These components can also provide strength during times of burnout. However, Maslach and Leiter conclude that when people continually bring burnout home, their exhaustion and negative feelings begin to affect relationships with family and friends (Maslach & Leiter, 1997, p. 19). This point of exhaustion leads some to search for rest and renewal.

When to Renew

While renewal comes in different forms for different people, there are some common factors or signs that can indicate when a person needs a period of renewal. According to O'Neil, one major factor is when a people come home from work physically, but psychologically and spiritually remain imprisoned by the roles they have created for themselves at work (O'Neil, 1993, p. 24). Multiple signs such as working as much from home after getting home, or constantly having to answer the phone for work related calls may be indicators. People may spend years climbing the ladder of success only to reach the top and find that it is leaning against the wrong wall (Parsons, 2007, p. 48). It is vital for leaders to be able to pause and monitor the events and places around them in order to ensure that they are climbing the right wall.

Willard concludes that the inability to find adequate answers in life leaves people rudderless in the flood of events, and people are at the mercy of whatever ideas as well as forces that come to bear upon them (Willard, 2002, p. 16). Fatigue can also become the product of a flood of events and is another indicator of when rest and renewal is needed. Wuellner contends that fatigue is deep and pervasive (Wuellner, 1998, p. 109). Bass determines that fatigue and stress can produce faulty decision making, absenteeism, irritability at work, and a confused appearance (Bass, 2008, p. 812). The ability to identify when a person needs to pause, rest, and renew is paramount to not being swept away in the flood of these life events. Renewal is considered by many to be the hidden key for a successful life. No one really starts out in life to fail. However, stress and burnout are becoming more commonplace today. At some point in the life of every individual and organization, the need for renewal becomes vital and even nature, itself, proclaims the need for periodic renewal to succeed (O'Neil, 1993, p. 122).

Guidelines for rest may be unique to given situations, but the requirement for rest and renewal should be emphasized across the organization.

Vanderpyl produced the following suggestions to form a baseline policy for rest and renewal (Vanderpyl, 2012):

- Create mandatory "no smart-phone" times with teams. Leaders must set this example themselves and enforce it with their team. For example, a leader could mandate no checking or sending e-mails between midnight and 6 a.m. and on Sundays.
- Ensure and enforce a mandatory "no contact" practice between employees and the office while they are on vacation. This would need to prevent employees from contacting the office for any reason, and prevent employees still working from contacting the vacationing employee while he or she is away. Again, leaders must set a firm example in their own actions.
- Find ways to creatively praise employees who ask for time off for special family events, rather than praising those who sacrifice family events for the sake of work projects. Occasional projects may interfere with family time, but that should be known as an exception, not the norm.
- Find reasons, when possible, to send employees home early at random times with the mandate to relax at home. Many times, sport coaches rest their star players in games at the end of the season when that game does not actually matter. Work tends to be cyclical throughout the year, with busy and less-busy times. Leaders could use those less-busy times to rest their employees in anticipation of upcoming busy times.

Stress Management

Sporadic patterns of rest and renewal can easily increase the amount of stress a leader feels. Stress management becomes a primary concern for these leaders. Maslach and Leiter conclude that the majority of the stress management techniques are mistakenly designed to change the individual rather than the situation (Maslach & Leiter, 1997, p. 70). McCall and Hollenbeck describe that stable personal life situations are essential in maintaining stress-resistant personal arrangements, usually family, that supports a commitment to work and dealing with complexity (McCall Jr. & Hollenbeck, 2002, p. 36). Stress management solutions are not necessarily easy or "quick win" solutions for an organization. According to Fletcher and Jones, a malfunctioning organizational culture will be reflected in such indicators as poor quality of work, low levels of commitment to the organization, individuals working below capacity, high levels of absenteeism, labor turnover, poor health, alcoholism, stress, and a poor safety record (Fletcher & Jones, 1992).

Bass cautions that a hasty change can produce a high level of stress and tension (Bass B. , 2008). Quick and easy solutions are not always enduring and productive solutions. Balance provides a much better approach to stress management. Covey calls this the Production/Production Capability Balance (Covey, 1989):

> Production is referred to as a useful product (either tangible or intangible) that is being produced. Production Capacity is the process or method in which that product is being produced. The product is usually a result that is either produced continually or on a regular basis thereby introducing the necessity of keeping P (Production) and PC (Production Capacity) in balance. True effectiveness is a function of two things: what is produced and the producing asset or capacity to produce.

According to Covey, when organizations fail to respect this balance, they decrease in organizational effectiveness, which can lead to stress, and he provides the following example from Aesop's fable of the goose that laid the golden eggs for his point (Covey, 1989):

> A man had the good fortune to possess a goose that laid a golden egg every day. Lucky though the man was, he soon began to think he was not getting rich fast enough, and, imagining the bird must be made of gold inside, he decided to kill it to secure the entire store of precious metal at once. But when he cut it open he found it was just like any other goose. Thus, he neither got rich all at once, as he had hoped, nor enjoyed any longer the daily addition to his wealth.

The point Covey makes with this story is that people must balance the production capability, or "PC" (in this case, the goose), to get the product, or the "P" (that is, the golden eggs). Just as the man in the fable didn't take care of his goose, leaders need to be careful not to ignore their health, family, relaxation, and religious activities by spending too much time and activity on work (Kaniss, 2006). Balancing production capability, product, and time away from work will help leaders balance stress management with life events. Block contends that the current mindset of modern society is a one-minute culture in which speed is God and time is the devil; the need for speed becomes an obstacle for real change and may only increase stress (Block, 2001). This type of drive produces stressful situations in the life of the leader and the organization. At this point, stress management of the organization becomes paramount instead of the stress managements solutions of the individual.

Scripture and Rest

Jesus also emphasized the need for rest as He went about introducing the Kingdom of God. Wright contends that Jesus introduces a counter-cultural movement during the Second Temple Period by going out among the people in the local villages and demonstrating the power of God through healings, miracles, signs, and wonders; he believes that Jesus was emphasizing that the Kingdom was at hand and all are invited to join (Wright, 1999). Jesus did not limit His expansion of the Kingdom just to the leaders of His day as He went about mingling with the common people and explaining to them in a simple practical way the duties of the Kingdom (Freeman, 1972). One aspect of the Kingdom that Jesus emphasized was the need for rest in Matthew 11:28-29 (HCSB, 2010):

> "Come to Me, all of you who are weary and burdened, and I will give you rest. All of you, take up My yoke and learn from Me, because I am gentle and humble in heart, and you will find rest for yourselves."

In this text, Jesus emphasizes that rest is found in Him by repeating it twice in two verses. According to France, Jesus is referencing rest at the true being of the person, so here the reference is to rest at the deepest level, which is to build a new relationship with God (France, 2007, Kindle Locations 8256-8260). True rest must extend into the spiritual part of a person as well as the physical part.

It is vital when climbing the ladder of success to pause, rest, and renew in order to ensure that the ladder is up against the correct wall. There is little value in getting to the top of the ladder only to find that it is leaning against the wrong wall. The stress and burn-out of the long hours will only lead to a life of loneliness and empty desires. Rest and renewal are critical competencies for innovative leaders to successfully thrive in today's environment. Faulty decision making and lack of productivity due to stress and burn-out will not lead to long successful careers. Rest and renewal need to be considered on a regular basis to ensure a proper balance in life's goals. Stop and plan today for a time of rest and renewal. The world and your workplace will be better off with this renewal.

Chapter 12 The Common Core of Leadership Succession

"Life is a succession of lessons which must be lived to be understood."
—Helen Keller

"Nature gives to every time and season some beauties of its own; and from morning to night, as from the cradle to the grave, it is but a succession of changes so gentle and easy that we can scarcely mark their progress."
—Charles Dickens

"One of the things we often miss in succession planning is that it should be gradual and thoughtful, with lots of sharing of information, and knowledge with perspective, so that it's almost a non-event when it happens."
—Anne M. Mulcahy, Former CEO Xerox

The common core of leadership succession may be one of the most overlooked competencies until leaders near the end of their tenure. However, successful leadership succession actually begins on day one. Finzel states that one of the top mistakes that leaders make is having success with a successor, and he concludes that leaders need to plan their departure on the day they begin (Finzel, 1994, p. 157). Therefore, innovative leaders need to develop a strategy for leadership succession. Bass explains that traditional succession strategies promote from within when potential successors are assessed, developed, and coached for numerous leadership positions with opportunities for internal and external training (Bass B.,

2008, p. 886). Rothwell contends that one of the keys to effective succession planning is communicating upward and laterally concerning management of the organization (Rothwell, 2005, p. 19). The future of many good organizations will be realized as leaders work hand-in-hand with others in the organization to produce a healthy climate of cooperation in succession planning. This is especially true for organizations that have transformational and/or charismatic leaders.

Transformation and Charismatic Leaders

The study of transformational and charismatic leadership is relatively recent, but the research has been steadily growing. Burns first introduced the transforming leader in 1978 when he concluded that transforming leadership was best built upon a relationship of mutual stimulation and elevation that converts followers into leaders and leaders into moral agents (Burns, 1978). While charismatic leadership can be regarded as part of transformational leadership, some research indicates that the undesirable consequences at the societal level of charismatic leadership include totalitarian aspects as well as truth manipulation practiced by some charismatic leaders (Aaltio-Marjosola & Takala, 2000).

Khurana issues a caution concerning charismatic-only leaders when he states that the charismatic succession process implies that a single individual deserves vastly more attention and rewards than anyone else in the organization, and ignores the reality that organizational performance is driven by more than one person (Khurana, 2002, p. 197). Bass relates the dynamics of the charismatic leader-follower relationship and concludes that charismatic leaders often use themselves as examples for their subordinates to follow (Bass B., 2008, p. 590). Khurana concludes that many organizations focus on the charisma of the organizational leader and seriously underestimate the risk of outside succession (Khurana, 2002, p. 188). Northouse identifies four specific types of charismatic behavior (Northouse, 2007, pp. 178-179):

- They are strong role models for the beliefs and values they want their followers to adopt.
- They appear competent to followers.

- They articulate ideological goals that have moral overtones.
- They communicate high expectations for followers and they exhibit confidence in their followers' abilities to meet these expectations.

Bass posits that charismatics can foster antisocial behavior, and personalized charismatic leaders can be dominant, self-interested, and authoritarian (Bass B., 2008, p. 578). While charismatic and transformational leadership styles are similar, there are some differences; especially when measured against the servant leadership style. According to Stone, Russell, and Patterson, transformational leaders direct their focus toward the organization, so their behavior builds follower commitment toward organizational objectives, while servant leaders focus on their followers, and the achievement of organizational objectives is a subordinate outcome (Stone, Russell, & Patterson, 2004). Kotter concludes that many organizations have a leadership deficit because the organization ignores the leadership potential in the members of that organization, thereby, not offering training or relevant role models to raise up leaders from within (Kotter, 2005). Deming outlines three steps to get others involved in accomplishing transformative change (Deming, 1994):

- The transformative leader has a theory and understands why the transformation would bring gains to the organization as well as to the people involved in the organization.
- The transformative leader feels compelled to accomplish the transformation as an obligation to the people and the organization.
- The transformative leader has a step-by-step plan and can explain it in simple terms.

A transformational leader can make the organization more successful by valuing its human capital. Northouse determines that the effect of organizational change through transformational leaders is the ability of the transformational leader to be a role model, create a vision, and empower followers to facilitate ownership of the process (Northouse, 2007). The Apostle John provides a good example of a transformational leader as the newly organized church prepares to enter the second century without any of their foundational leaders.

Early Church Leadership Succession

The Book of Revelation is generally acknowledged as the primary eschatological book of the Bible. However, DeSilva advances the thought that the Book of Revelation should be exegetically analyzed according to its original audience. He contends that John's fantastic images invite Christians living in the Roman province of Asia Minor during the last decade of the first century to perceive the true character of the realities that face them every day, and to respond to them in a manner that will allow them to share in the triumph of the Lamb rather than in the punishment of Rome (DeSilva, 2004, p. 885). Following this vein of thought, the letter to the Church of Philadelphia can be analyzed according to the premise of the day to understand how the Apostle John was trying to move the church away from the Second Temple Period of Judaism by identifying their unique strengths and move the church into the future by recognizing seven new leaders in seven geographic locations in Revelation chapters two and three. As the last of the original twelve apostles, John had the unique role of developing leadership succession after all of the original apostles were gone. No other leader in the history of the church had more at stake in leadership succession than John.

A sacred texture analysis of the Letter to the Church at Philadelphia in Revelation 3:7-13 reveals that John was using the concept of mentoring in the formation and nurturing of this religious community as well as the preparation for the young pastors from these seven churches to continue the work of the ministry. Jesus mentored the 12 original Apostles to continue His work, and John is mentoring the pastors in the seven churches identified in Revelation to continue that work. In light of these examples, the Christian ethical response to succession planning is to work with the next generation of leaders and mentor them based upon their strengths to continue the work. Additional analysis provides context for modern day leaders moving their organizations into the future through the creative use of strength based leadership and mentoring for developing a leadership succession program.

Sacred Texture

According to Robbins and his Socio-Rhetorical Interpretation model, sacred texture is the fifth of five textures. Robbins concludes that a sacred text features one or more people who have a special relationship to God, and the holy person par excellence in the New Testament is Jesus the Christ, which is regularly identified from New Testament texts as Christology (Robbins, 1996, p. 121). A common theme in the ministry of Jesus was His introduction of the Kingdom of God. Wright contends that Jesus introduced a counter-cultural movement during the Second Temple Period by going out among the people in the local villages and demonstrating the power of God through healings, miracles, signs, and wonders; he believes that Jesus was emphasizing that the kingdom was at hand and all were invited to join (Wright, 1999). This is the pinnacle of leadership succession, which is leading a large group of people into the future and away from the traditions of the past that no longer work. Then develop a system of mentoring the successive leaders to continue that work. Another aspect of the sacred texture is the formation and nurturing of a religious community (Robbins, 1996, p. 127).

Gyertson defines the real purpose and power of the church as redemption and that Scripture was not just for the personal needs of a troubled runaway life, but actually the life source for the problems and critical issues that have plagued people from the beginning of time to the present day (Gyertson, 1993, p. 11). Yet, to join this kingdom required a change—a uniquely creative change—now commonly called salvation. However, the first introduction of salvation was NOT commonly understood. Jesus told Nicodemus in John 3:3 that unless someone is born again, he cannot see the Kingdom of God (HCSB, 2010). Yet, Nicodemus could not understand this innovative change process. Jesus did not limit His expansion of the Kingdom just to the leaders of His day as He went about mingling with the common people and explaining to them in a simple practical way the duties of the Kingdom (Freeman, 1972). By the time that John writes his letter to the Church at Philadelphia, Jerusalem is gone and the Kingdom of God has expanded through the diaspora. Of the original 12 Apostles only John is left, and he understands the need to mentor young pastors to expand the kingdom after he is gone. Just as Jesus empowered the 12

Apostles to continue the work of the Kingdom, John is empowering the local pastors of the seven churches of Revelation 2-4 to continue their work of the Kingdom.

The Church at Philadelphia

To develop an understanding of the formation and nurturing of the religious community at the church in Philadelphia during the time of John, and the letter that he writes to that church, requires a background study into that area. Ancient Philadelphia is known as Alaşehir, Turkey today and was a Lydian city founded by Attalus II Philadelphus (220-130 BC) who was known for his devotion to his brother Eumenes (Halley, 1980, p. 698). Philadelphia was a city of commercial importance, conveniently located as the gateway to the high central plateau of the Roman province of Asia in Asia Minor and was an outpost of Hellenism in native Anatolia. Built upon a major fault line, Philadelphia suffered a massive earthquake in AD 17 and was tormented by 20 years of recurrent quakes, which caused many people to move outside of the city for several years (Archaeological Study Bible NIV, 2005, pp. 2050-2051). The pastor of the church at Philadelphia has distinctive needs to expand the Kingdom of God due to the unique circumstances of this area. John uses an approach of identifying the unique needs and circumstances of each of these seven churches, and then turning that situation into a kingdom expansion leadership succession project through mentoring. The sacred texture analysis of Revelation 3:12 uncovers John's mentoring message to this community and its pastor (HCSB, 2010):

> The victor: I will make him a pillar in the sanctuary of My God, and he will never go out again. I will write on him the name of My God and the name of the city of My God—the New Jerusalem, which comes down out of heaven from My God—and My new name.

Due to the earthquake tendencies in this area, the people are constantly moving in and out of the city. Uncertainty and instability become commonplace. Therefore, John is combating this community challenge by proclaiming that the Lord will make each of them a pillar of stability in this church and they will not have to move in-and-out any longer. The

Kingdom of God is theirs and is built upon their lives. This custom of writing names on pillars was commonplace. In the ruins of the synagogue in Capernaum there are two pillars with dedicatory inscriptions which indicate that the custom of writing on the columns of buildings was quite common (Baez-Camargo, 1986, p. 264). Additionally, Scottish archaeologist and New Testament scholar William Mitchell Ramsay concludes that the "new name" imagery of verse 12 is certainly a reference to the proposal to rename the city "Neocaesarea" in gratitude for Tiberius' generous earthquake relief (Archaeological Study Bible NIV, 2005, p. 2050). Even today, churches put the names of people on bricks or on pews to honor and commemorate their service to the church. Cities will even name buildings and schools after prominent leaders in their community. John is identifying the unique characteristics and strengths of this community to build his leadership succession program for this pastor to carry on the work of the ministry after John is gone. This type of identification of strengths based leadership can be used for organizations today to build mentoring programs for leadership succession.

Application & Analysis for Today

Analyzing the Seven Letters to the Churches in general and the letter to the Church Of Philadelphia in specific from the formation and nurturing of the religious community perspective with Robbins' Sacred Texture reveals that the Apostle John intended to identify with the unique strengths and circumstances of this community and to use those strengths to move the community, as well as the church, forward with successive leaders. Through the creative identification of unique strengths and circumstances in each church, John begins to mentor these pastors to move them away from the Second Temple period and direct their attention to the future establishment of their church and people. A key component for leadership successive programs is to develop a "futures" mentality. Organizations of today can learn from these letters by John and establish a culture to identify their strength's to lead them into mentoring relationships to develop a leadership succession program.

Bell indicates that the challenge for all learning facilitators is the actual transfer of learning (Bell C. R., 2002, p. 133). This is true for establishing leadership succession principles and traits. The Apostle John uses the creative identification of unique strengths in each of the Seven Churches in the Book of Revelation to identify a common ground for developing new leaders from these pastors of the Seven Churches in Asia Minor to continue the work of the ministry after he is gone. While the Apostolic ministry continues today, the last original Apostle has passed the leadership mantle for the local church to the local pastors.

Organizations of today can use choose to follow this pattern. It is vital for leaders of today to creatively identify the unique strengths of their organization and start the leadership succession process as soon as possible. Rothwell identifies that one of the ten key trends on succession planning and management is the importance of values and competencies (Rothwell, 2005, p. 42). Therefore, the innovative leaders' response to succession planning is to identify the next generation of leaders and develop them based upon their unique strengths to continue the work.

Chapter 13 The Common Core of Mentoring & Discipleship

"Tell me and I forget, teach me and I may remember,
involve me and I learn."
—Benjamin Franklin

"The 'show business,' which is so incorporated into our view of Christian work today, has caused us to drift far from Our Lord's conception of discipleship. It is instilled in us to think that we have to do exceptional things for God; we have not. We have to be exceptional in ordinary things, to be holy in mean streets, among mean people, surrounded by sordid sinners. That is not learned in five minutes."
—Oswald Chambers

"The pen is mightier than the sword."
—Edward Bulwer-Lytton

Words are powerful. In 1839, Edward Bulwer-Lytton coins the phrase for a play which says, "The pen is mightier than the sword." However, the thought was not unique to him. As early as 406 BC, the Greek poet Euripides said, "The tongue is mightier than the blade." Pre-dating all that is Genesis 1:3 when the Lord demonstrates the true power of words and SAID, "Let there be light," and there was light. Two words that contain infinite power for innovative leaders are discipling and mentoring.

Words of Action and Change

Mentoring and discipling are two words of action and change. Their reach is beyond time and space. However, these words are not interchangeable and will produce different results. According to Bell, mentoring focuses on helping others learn (Bell C. R., 2002, p. 5). Bekker extends that concept to conclude that mentoring is follower-centric (Leadership Talks, 2007). Mentoring is based upon relationship and focuses on leaders working with followers to be all that they can be (Puryear, 2002, p. 189). The mentor's goal is to help followers accomplish the followers' plans.

Discipling produces a different outcome. Winston defines discipling as leader-centric where a person is learning from the leader and wants to be like the leader (Leadership Talks, 2007). Under this banner, followers may give up their own personal plan to take on the vision or purpose of the leader. Jesus told His followers in Matthew 28:19 to go and make disciples. Discipling is leader-centric and focuses on the followers becoming like the leader in some area of their life. As emerging innovative leaders, it takes wisdom to be able to determine which role to use in developing followers. Both roles are valuable, but produce different outcomes.

Discipling Transcends Time and Space

The Apostle Paul encourages believers in I Corinthians 11:1 to "imitate me just as I also imitate Christ (Spirit Filled Life Bible (NKJV), 1991)." Paul understood the need for discipleship in the lives of his followers and wants them to become like him. Bekker recognizes four important aspects of discipleship (Leadership Talks, 2007):

- Followers must desire to learn and be like the master or leader.
- Followers must say no to their own plans and die to self.
- Followers take up the vision of the leader.
- Followers take up the quest of the leader.

Winston adds that discipling does not need to be a face-to-face encounter (Leadership Talks, 2007). He describes a self-study process that he went through with W. Edwards Deming and found that he wanted to be like him in some areas. Even though he had never met Deming, he found himself being "discipled" by Deming's work. In the same manner, Paul is still discipling believers today through the documents that he left behind.

Discipling produces a different outcome. Again, discipling is leader-centric where a person is learning from the leader (or master) and wants to be like the leader. Therefore, followers give up their plans in order to take on the vision or purpose of the leader. This can be seen in Scripture where Jesus told His followers to go and make disciples in Matthew 28:16-20 (Spirit Filled Life Bible (NKJV), 1991):

> Then the eleven disciples went away into Galilee, to the mountain which Jesus had appointed for them. When they saw Him, they worshiped Him; but some doubted. And Jesus came and spoke to them, saying, "All authority has been given to Me in heaven and on earth. Go therefore and make disciples of all the nations, baptizing them in the name of the Father and of the Son and of the Holy Spirit, teaching them to observe all things that I have commanded you; and lo, I am with you always, even to the end of the age."

The Greek word used here for "disciples" is *mathetes* which is used over 250 times in the New Testament (Wigram, 1979, pp. 466-468). According to Bekker, *mathetes* is like an apprentice in modern times (Leadership Talks, 2007). These followers of Jesus served as His apprentices. Again, both roles are valuable, but produce different outcomes. Mentoring produces a diverse group of people each accomplishing their own vision and purpose; discipling produces a group which looks, speaks, and acts the same as they pursue a common vision.

Mentoring: Face-to-Face Encounters

On the other hand, mentoring requires more of a face-to-face encounter. Since mentoring relies upon relationship, there is an implication of time being spent with the person being mentored. General Dwight Eisenhower was once asked by Edgar Puryear how a person can be developed as a decision maker. The General replied that the key was to be around people who made decisions and rely on them as mentors (Puryear, 2002, p. 188). Hendricks claims that the mentoring relationship is about becoming a marked man and focuses on helping people (Hendricks & Hendricks, 1995, p. 13). Leaders are to mark and make a significant impact on their followers. Mentoring requires that one-on-one time to be effective. However, discipling can be accomplished through the study of the documents left behind. Mentoring and discipling are important measures or competencies to build innovative leaders and teams.

Teamwork

Teamwork is a key enabler for organizations. Bass states that in designing an organization a balance needs to be struck among three variables: centralized control, decentralized autonomy, and cooperative teamwork; control and cooperation need to be balanced between consistency and flexibility (Bass B., 2008, p. 738). Bossidy identifies that an essential behavior for leaders is to know your people and know your business in order to successfully change organizational plans and structures (Bossidy & Charan, 2002). Cooperative teamwork helps to produce an environment where people know each other and work together to make a difference. Deming states that the idea that competition is a necessary way of life needs to be discarded and replaced with the idea of cooperation because, over time, competition squeezes out the innate intrinsic motivation, self-esteem, and dignity of an individual and then replaces it with fear, self-defense, and extrinsic motivation (Deming, 1994).

Bennis claims that a shrinking world in which technological and political complexity increase at an accelerating rate offers fewer arenas in which individual action and top-down leadership suffices (Bennis, 2000). The future of many good organizations will be realized as leaders work hand-in-hand with others in the organization to produce a healthy climate of cooperation. Replacing a competitive organizational structure with a more productive cooperative environment is not just a Bennis and Deming idea for North America. As previously mentioned, research in China contends that productivity and people maintenance values have traditionally been considered to contribute to leadership effectiveness and cooperative rather than competitive goal interdependence mediates the relationship between these values and outcomes (Liu, Yu, & Tjosvold, 2002). Cooperative teamwork build unity in an organization.

Team Building and the Power of Unity

Team building and the power of unity are amazing forces in an organization. Tushman and O'Reilly state that the implementation of change is enhanced when groups work together (Tushman & O'Reilly, 2002, p. 116). One of the first recorded instances of group work can be found in the Old Testament at the Tower of Babel in Genesis 11:6 which records that The LORD said, "If they have begun to do this as one people all having the same language, then nothing they plan to do will be impossible for them (HCSB, 2010)." Ancient cities were dominated by a temple complex, including a tower, and the typical Mesopotamian temple tower, known as a ziggurat, was square at the base; the sides were sloped and stepped that led upward to a small shrine at the top where the particular deity would descend to receive worship (Archaeological Study Bible NIV, 2005, p. 20). While the creation of this ziggurat was a remarkable achievement, the Lord was not pleased with this temple as He confused the languages and scattered the people.

This power of unity works for modern day organizations as well. When former Disney CEO Michael Eisner realized that his top executives would work better if they were developed as a team, he instituted a program called Disney Dimensions for his top team, which he dubbed his synergy boot camp (Woolfe, 2002, p. 140). For eight days, these executives experienced every aspect of the theme park where they made the beds in the hotels, worked in the kitchen, cleaned bathrooms, cut hedges, checked out guests, and soothed tired children. The executives keep up this routine from 7:00 A.M. to 11:00 P.M. for over a week and this experience forged them into a team that willingly, even enthusiastically, sacrificed individual ego for the unity and goals of the group (Eisner, 1998, p. 237).

Mentoring: A 2000 Year Old Leadership Principle

Mentoring is firmly based upon establishing relationships. A classic example would be the Apostle Paul mentoring his young protégée, Timothy, and leaving him to fulfill the work in Ephesus. Paul is very close to this family and has known them for many years. Paul has worked hard over the years to mentor and disciple this young man. When Paul nears the completion of his work, he wants to impart wisdom in training the next generation of leaders. In Ephesus, Timothy eventually leads this church and carries on the work of his great mentor. Paul used mentoring to release the anointing and creativity in Timothy to complete his work in Ephesus.

Understanding a 2000 year old leadership principle that still works today would be valuable to modern global leaders. The Apostle Paul demonstrated this leadership tool throughout his life and ministry. Paul effectively employed the leadership tool of mentoring as he developed and expanded the church across cultural, political, economic, and social boundaries. The ideological texture developed by Robbins can be used to identify Paul's employment of mentoring to resolve the challenges that he encountered and overcame, which are similar to those faced by leaders today in an increasingly global environment. Paul knew that his time was limited and he must prepare his young pastors to continue the work after he was gone. Many times, dynamic mega-churches dwindle away after the charismatic founding pastor is no longer the leader. Corporations often struggle when a long-time leader steps down. Paul has much to teach the innovative leaders of today.

Paul, like Jesus, understood the principle of mentoring and wanted to ensure that the new Christian leaders were prepared to carry on without him. Just as Jesus trained up His followers, Paul is doing likewise. According to Briner and Pritchard, Jesus actually trained and prepared the most successful leadership team of all time (Briner & Pritchard, 1998, p. 170). As the old saying goes, "the proof is in the pudding". The disciples went from a group of eleven to a current worldwide "organization" of billions. DeSilva noted that the letters to Timothy and Titus stand out among the letters written by Paul in that they were addressed to Paul's coworkers and delegates rather than a church (DeSilva, 2004, p. 733). Mentoring relationships are a vital component of successful leadership. Paul understood the necessity of mentoring leaders to continue his work after he was gone. In 2 Timothy 2:2, Paul identifies that mentoring should be started with faithful men. Robbins would identify 2 Timothy 2:2 as the conversionist response which, as previously stated, is characterized by a view that the world is corrupt because people are corrupt and if people can be changed, the world will be changed (Robbins, 1996, p. 72).

Ideological Texture

According to Robbins and his Socio-Rhetorical Interpretation model, ideological texture is the fourth of five textures. According to Robbins, the ideological texture begins with people, and he defines ideology as an integrated system of beliefs, assumptions, and values (Robbins, 1996, p. 96). It is concerned with the alliance and conflicts within the language of the text as well as the way the text and its interpreters position themselves relative to other individuals and groups in that time. The individual locations sub-texture is the first step toward ideological texture analysis. It is characterized by the individuals' involved in the texts' responses to the world as well as the individuals' cultural location. Robbins uses the ideological texture to focus on the socio-cultural background and individual location as well as the perspective of the writers and readers of the text (Robbins, 1996, p. 95). DeSilva identifies that ideological texture recognizes that a text is not just a vehicle for ideas, but a vehicle by which the author hopes to achieve a certain goal (DeSilva, 2004, p. 25). Luke starts off Acts 1:8 with his version of the Great Commission and then provides substantial detail about Paul's efforts to fulfill that commission through his travels. Many of these early churches were small house-groups, led by people who had heard the gospel (Elwell & Yarbrough, 1998, p. 340). As the author of the Book of Acts, Luke identifies that Paul stays in Corinth for 18 months (Acts 18:11). While this Scripture is easy to pass over, it underscores Paul's global strategy of establishing churches by spending a significant amount of time immersed in the local culture. According to Robbins, ideological criticism is closely tied to the investigation of the social location in regard to the text (Robbins, 1996, p. 118). As the capital of Achaia, Corinth is a bustling port city, and it is the center of worship to the goddess, Aphrodite (Hayford, 1995).

Corinth is well-known as a place of immorality and paganism. However, Paul determines to win this city to the Lord during his extended stay. The opposition to his ministry is so fierce that Jesus appears to Paul in a vision to encourage him (Acts 18:9). Paul understands that changing the culture of Corinth is going to take time and patience. Two of his longest letters (1 and 2 Corinthians) further emphasize his commitment to this community. DeSilva confirms that Paul was brought up on charges before the Roman proconsul of Achaia, Lucius Junius Gallio, which connects these events to the year of 51 C.E. (DeSilva, 2004, p. 489). Corinth provides some of Paul's strongest opposition, but he is determined to establish the gospel in this area.

Paul's Use of Mentoring

Similar to Corinth, Paul moves to Ephesus and continues there for three years. Some cultural background information is necessary to fully understand and appreciate the richness of the Ephesians text. The grand and glorious city of Ephesus was the capital of the Roman province of Asia, which is now part of western Turkey (Elwell & Yarbrough, 1998, p. 308). When the Apostle Paul first visited this city around 52-55 AD, he found a large city filled with fame, power, superstition and sin with its greatest claim to fame being the grandiose temple of Artemis (also called Diana) which was one of the seven wonders of the ancient world (Ludwig, 1983, p. 153). In addition to Paul, Timothy plays an important part in the growth of the Ephesian's church. His mother and grandmother were probably born again under Paul's first missionary journey to Lystra (Hayford, 1995, p. 412). Seven years later, Paul returns to Lystra to find Timothy fervently working in the church. He eventually travels with Paul and is sent to Ephesus where he becomes the first Bishop of Ephesus (Hayford, 1995). Additionally, he is very close to this family and he has known them for many years. Paul has worked hard over the years to mentor and disciple this young man. When Paul nears the completion of his work, he wants to impart wisdom in training up the next generation of leaders. In Ephesus, Timothy eventually leads this church and carries on the work of his great mentor. In addition to Timothy and Paul being in Ephesus, church tradition indicates that John's gospel was written in Ephesus around 95 A.D. (DeSilva, 2004). Since Timothy was martyred in 97 A.D., he was probably still in Ephesus during this time (St. Timothy's Church, 2007). The seeds of leadership that Paul was sowing into the life of Timothy led Ephesus to become a center for the church after the fall of Jerusalem and before the church finally settles in Rome.

False teachers had crept in to the church and were threatening the stability and integrity of the early church (Elwell & Yarbrough, 1998). Paul wants to prepare young Timothy to counter this threat. In Paul's letters to Timothy he is explaining to him that he is capable of leading the congregation in Ephesus, and he trusts him completely. In I Timothy 1:3, Paul urges him to stay in Ephesus to charge or command some to teach no other doctrine (Spirit Filled Life Bible (NKJV), 1991). Even at this early stage, Paul is encouraging his young mentor to begin mentoring. When Paul lists the characteristics of an overseer in I Timothy 3:2-7, he is instructing Timothy that he already has these traits of leadership. Paul states that overseers are to have these characteristics and by virtue of Paul setting Timothy as an overseer in Ephesus, he already has them. Timothy is charged with the development of more teachers to teach along these same lines. Paul emphasizes the need for sound instruction in I Timothy 4:11 when he charges Timothy again to command and teach to confront the error that was creeping into the church at Ephesus. According to DeSilva, the author of Timothy is very concerned about the preservation of the Pauline gospel (DeSilva, 2004, p. 737).

Mentoring for Today's Leaders

Mentoring relationships are methods directed toward change, and mentoring is a relationship oriented process. Bell defines mentoring as a learning process whereby the mentor teaches or guides the less learned (Bell C. R., 2002, p. 3). The focus is on the follower becoming more competent by virtue of learning and practicing. According to Zachary, many employees often seek guidance from a senior person in their organization, but are deeply disappointed with the lack of mentoring relationships; such disappointments often lead to staff turnover (Zachary, 2005). To establish a successful mentoring program that can be used globally, organizations can look at producing a model or compatible program which can be used. Bell introduces the SAGE model for mentoring (Surrendering, Accepting, Gifting, and Extending) (Bell C. R., 2002, p. 14):

- *Surrendering (S)* is all about actions that make mentoring a power-free experience. We have learned that power, authority, and command—or at least the protégé's perception of these traits in the mentor—can doom the mentoring experience to a perfunctory dialogue... sans risks, sans spirit, and sans discovery.

- *Accepting (A)* in the SAGE model focuses on the value of a safe, nontoxic relationship. When the protégé believes he or she is in a relationship that is not dangerous, growth-producing risk and experimentation are more likely to occur. The perception or prediction of danger is related not to physical harm but rather to the emotional damage caused by rebuke, judgment, or criticism—all of which yield a loss of protégé self-esteem in front of an important person. Why is this important? Without risk there is no learning; without experimentation there is no progress.
- *Gifting (G)* is positioned as the main event in mentoring. Many mentors start their mentoring relationships with a gift of advice, feedback, or focus. However, when offered as the first step in the relationship, the act of bestowing such gifts risks their being at best undervalued, at worst ignored, resisted, or rejected. If Gifting follows Surrendering and Accepting, it is more likely to be experienced by the protégé as a sincere gesture and a valued contribution worthy of attention, tryout, and effort.
- *Extending (E)* in the SAGE is about the creation and nurturance of the protégé as a self-directed learner. It is also about ways to extend the learning of the protégé beyond his or her relationship with the mentor. Essentially, it is shepherding the transfer of learning.

Gregson categorizes the various aspects of starting a mentoring culture to include deciding on objectives as well as selection, training, and matching mentors to certain junior staff (Gregson, 1994). Mentoring programs that focus upon relationship building should provide a good cross-cultural solution. However, this requires the mentor to have regular face-to-face sessions with the follower. The mentoring process needs time for the relationship to develop and the process to work through a multitude of issues. Major General (retired) William Cohen defines mentoring as taking care of your people, which he calls the Sixth Universal Law of Leadership (Cohen W. A., 1998).

Again, Bell indicates that the challenge for all learning facilitators is the actual transfer of learning (Bell C. R., 2002, p. 133). This is true for mentoring as well as establishing a common core of competencies for emerging innovative leaders. Paul uses mentoring to train up his young pastors to continue the work of the ministry after he is gone. Paul also continues to disciple Christians through the letters he wrote during his life. It is vital for leaders to start the mentoring or discipling process as soon as possible in order to spend as much time as needed and complete the tasks at hand of working with, as well as understanding, people.

Chapter 14
The Common Core of Understanding People

"Those who know, do. Those that understand, teach."
—Aristotle

"Wisdom is the principal thing; Therefore, get wisdom.
And in all your getting, get understanding."
Proverbs 4:7

While ethics may be the most complex common core for innovative leaders, understanding people could be the most difficult. Understanding people may be accomplished through studying human behavior –preferences, avoidances, motivations, responses, etc. Carbonell states that the study of personalities is called the study of human behavior (Carbonell, 1993). Bass correlates personalities into two overall leadership styles: task-oriented and relations-oriented (Bass B., 2008). Hersey and Blanchard contend that structure (task) and consideration (relationships) are the two most important leadership dimensions in describing how a leader performs and concludes that high ratings on both dimensions characterize effective or desirable leadership (Hersey & Blanchard, 1969).

Bennis claims that the new reality is that intellectual capital, brain power, know-how, and human imagination has supplanted monetary capital as the critical success factor and leaders will have to learn an entirely new set of skills that are not understood, not taught in our business schools, and, for all of those reasons, rarely practiced (Bennis, 1999). Task-oriented and relations-oriented leadership styles are part of this reality that Bennis references. As innovative leaders begin to look inward for ways to move and motivate people rather than looking outward for new programs or the latest fads, the development, expansion, and maturity of their leadership styles come into focus. According to Hersey and Blanchard, depending on the maturity of subordinates, a manager should be task-oriented and tell or sell subordinates regarding what to do; or a manager should be relations-oriented and participate with subordinates in joint decision making; or the decisions should be delegated to them (Hersey & Blanchard, 1969).

Task Oriented or Relations Oriented

Bass claims that powerful autocratic or task-oriented leaders throughout history have often been praised for their ability to develop reliable and devoted followers and to act as the principal authority figures in establishing and maintaining order (Bass B., 2008, p. 440). A common perception is that leaders who are more task-oriented will achieve higher levels of task accomplishment. However, no differences were found in performance when leaders evidenced a more relationship-oriented style of leadership (Tabernero, Chambel, Curral, & Arana, 2009). Which leadership style works best may depend on the leader and the followers. However, as Plato observed, there may be no time for a democratic vote on a ship in a storm. Bass further determines that most executives who make it to the top of their organizations are task-oriented, but many are also inclined to be concerned with their relationships (Bass B., 2008, p. 497). He also contends that leaders have to be strong and decisive, yet sensitive to the needs of the followers. Even though only two leadership styles seem to be prevalent in research, there are many different expressions of these styles.

The relations-oriented style may be active or passive. Where an active relations style is expressive, demonstrative, inspirational, influential, and impressive towards a group, the passive expression becomes more focused on individual people and prefers to work one-on-one or in small groups. Many times, the more active personalities will take the credit for much of the work completed by people with a passive or reserved style. However, the passive style would strongly prefer NOT to be in the limelight or get any of the attention. Their quiet nature leads them to be more thoughtful and intuitive of people. The passive or reserved relations-oriented leader prefers a steady pace, security, and does not like sudden change. These leaders are calm, relaxed, patient, possessive, predictable, deliberate, stable, consistent, and tend to be unemotional and poker-faced. These leaders are not strong task-oriented people. Their strength is in looking out for others. They are much more interested in the general welfare of the people in the group rather than actually getting the work done.

The task-oriented leadership style can also be active or passive (reserved). The active style is more demanding, dominating, and decisive. However, the passive expression of task-oriented leaders becomes more cautious, calculating, compliant to their own standards, and prefers a checklist of items to be accomplished. The active leader may have to help these people with the list, but once it has been developed they will work tirelessly and efficiently in completing the list.

One of the roles in the mentoring or discipling process is to develop a team to work together in order to accomplish a goal or task. It is the function of the leader to move that group from the unknown parts of the task to the known and accomplished parts. Effective leaders will select the best team members. This is where the initial challenge begins. The most difficult part of accomplishing a task or goal is not the actual work involved, nor is it merely the identification of the task or goal. The most difficult part is the one that is often overlooked—selecting the team.

Too many times, the membership of a team is simply who is present at the time. Many times, leaders will simply survey the room, pick the people that they like (or are like them) and form the team, which is then sent out to accomplish working together to develop a solution or accomplish a task. However, a reliable system is a better alternative to the best guess method. Just as team has four letters, the key to putting together a successful team has four letters: DISC. The DISC form of understanding people is not a new concept; it has been around for many years.

DISC Model

As early as 400 BC, Hippocrates notes that four basic elements of nature could be identified as humors and ties them to personal behavioral patterns in people (LaHaye, 1983). Several hundred years later around 190 AD, a

Greek physician named Galenus of Pergamum, who is better known as Galen, recognizes four common temperaments. Galen names these four temperaments or personality patterns as choleric, sanguine, phlegmatic, and melancholy (Littauer & Littauer, 2006). Other studies map four types of animals, four types of strategies, four types of attitudes, four types of characters, four types of world views—even four types of thinking. Most studies always find four types of behavioral patterns. The DISC model of personality behavior builds upon these. The DISC model is the acronym for (Carbonell, 1993):

- Dominance – relating to control, power and assertiveness.
- Influence – relating to social situations and communication.
- Steadiness – relating to patience, persistence, and thoughtfulness.
- Conscientiousness – relating to structure and organization.

The original DISC Assessment Model was developed by John Geier and was based on the 1928 work of psychologist William Moulton Marston (Carbonell, 1993). DISC is the four quadrant behavioral model developed to examine the patterns of behavior for understanding people in specific situations. Most people will express or blend two of the four styles in varying degrees. Although all four contribute to the overall final expression, these blends start with the primary (or stronger) type, followed by the secondary (or lesser) type (Parsons, 2012).

These four areas of the DISC model closely correspond to Hippocrates original description of humors. Additionally, they can be grouped in a grid with "D" and "I" sharing the top row and representing outgoing or extroverted aspects of a person's behavior, while the "C" and "S" represent a passive or introverted aspect. "D" and "C" represent task-focused aspects, and "I" and "S" represent social aspects. A simple matrix can better explain (Carbonell, 1993):

The system identifying dimensions of observable behavior has become known as the universal language of behavior. DISC research has found that characteristics of behavior can be grouped into these four major behavioral styles or expressions, and they tend to exhibit specific characteristics common to that particular style. All individuals will operate or express all four types of patterns, but what differs from one to another is the extent of each (Parsons, 2012).

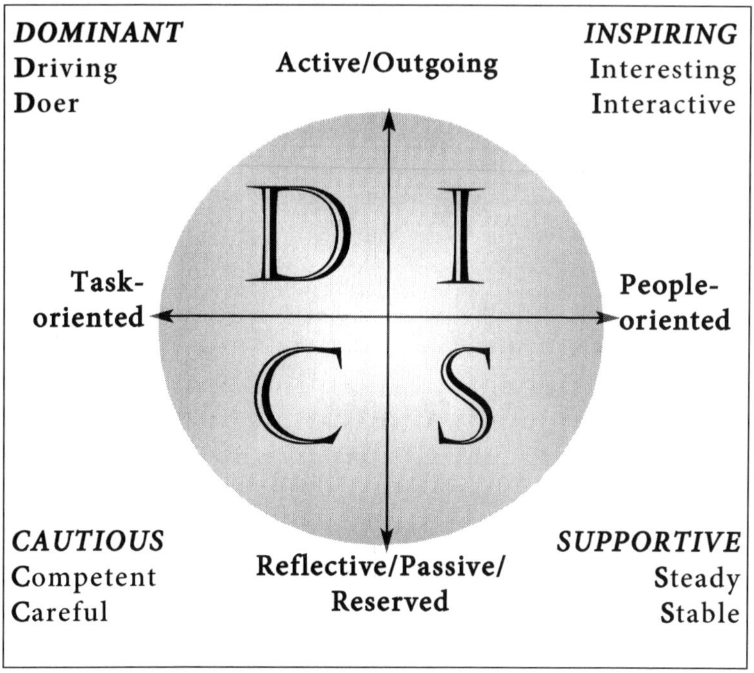

DISC Model graph by Carbonell

Understanding the differences between these blends makes it possible to integrate individual team members with less troubleshooting. In a typical team, there are varying degrees of compatibility, not just toward tasks, but interpersonal relationships as well. However, when they are identified, energy can be spent on refining the results. Each of these types adds its own unique value to the team, general characteristics, ideal environment, what the individual is motivated by, and value to the team. To create the most effective team is to bring together all four elements of the DISC model. Each member will have a purpose and role on the team. Always strengthen your strengths and staff your weaknesses in the team development process (Parsons, 2012). Team building begins with adding the missing personality pieces.

DISC Types: D—Direct and Demanding

The "D" type person is closely related to the Type "A" personality. This personality can be very demanding, direct, and dominating. No challenge is too big and no obstacle is too hard to overcome. Persistence and determination become common characteristics. They love a challenge and love to challenge anything and everything. For this person, the status quo only exists to be changed and re-created. The Apostle Paul demonstrates this type of personality. People who are high in their intensity of the "D" style are active in dealing with problems and challenges, while low "D's" are people who want to do more research before committing to a decision. High "D" people are described as demanding, forceful, egocentric, strong-willed, driving, determined, ambitious, aggressive, and pioneering.

In contrast to that, people who score more as a low "D" are described as those who are conservative, low-key, cooperative, calculating, undemanding, cautious, mild, agreeable, modest, and peaceful. High "D" personalities are people that change the world around them. They make great entrepreneurs as well as world class criminals. Statements such as, "My way or the highway" are commonplace. They are movers and doers. This personality is active towards tasks; however, they don't specialize in task completion. These people will have ten ongoing tasks and will be ready to take on more. Their greatest challenge is to focus on completing a task prior to starting a new one. They are goal-oriented, but will seldom take the time to write things down. All of their plans exist in their head, not on paper. They like to "shoot from the hip" and ask questions later. They will ask for forgiveness after the fact, rather than permission up-front.

Hand these people a task and they will quickly start the process. While they are not always seen as a team player, their value to the team is to get things started and moving; they help overcome inertia. This personality does not like to work in a closely supervised environment as this will quench their ideas and actions. A "D" type personality does not have, use, or think they need any social interaction skills. For them, it is all about the tasks—not the people. They have a tendency to be explosive and afterwards take you to the best restaurant in town for lunch as if nothing ever happened. They are always moving forward. What happened in the past is behind them. Their mind is already on the future.

A "D" leader must realize that people are important, and tasks need to be completed. This type of person enjoys starting tasks and will easily have many different projects going at once. Finishing projects or tasks is not one of their strong points. It is important to remember to focus on one task at a time and bring it to completion. The Apostle Paul is this type of leader, but realizes that he must learn to focus on completing one thing at a time in Philippians 3:12-14 (Spirit Filled Life Bible (NKJV), 1991):

> Not that I have already attained, or am already perfected; but I press on, that I may lay hold of that for which Christ Jesus has also laid hold of me. Brethren, I do not count myself to have apprehended; but one thing I do, forgetting those things which are behind and reaching forward to those things which are ahead, I press toward the goal for the prize of the upward call of God in Christ Jesus.

"D's" must learn to come under authority and work within the established guidelines. They don't play well with others, and they do not like their decisions challenged. However, given the proper information and options, they will change a decision at a moment's notice. They believe that a decision is made to be changed, and the only purpose for a plan is to have something to change! They are spontaneous and work well under pressure. Actually, pressure simply becomes a catalyst to start more tasks. Many times, they become the "go-to" person because of their ability to get things started. This personality is hard-driving and hard charging. They will often run over people to get the task started and to keep the task moving forward.

Their greatest strength is also their greatest weakness. The strength of persistence and determination will cause a "D" personality to look, and perhaps become, arrogant and self-willed. To guide a "D" personality towards maturity requires tempering persistence with discipline and to match determination with empathy. It is important for "D's" to be able to sincerely show care and compassion when working with people. It is vital to remember that people are NOT tools to use in completing a task, but those people are valuable and important.

D

DOMINANT, DIRECT, DEMANDING, DOING & DRIVING

ACTIVE & TASK-ORIENTED

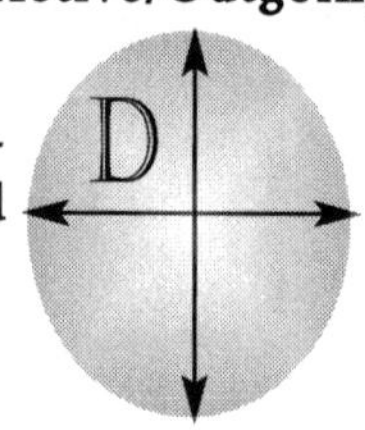

Greatest Strength:
Getting a task started

Greatest Fear:
Being embarrassed

Greatest Challenges:
Not finishing tasks
Submitting to authority

Bible Example:
Paul

Need to focus on:
The value of others
Finishing Tasks

DISC Types: I—Inspiring and Influential

In addition to the "D," the "I" personality is also very active. Whereas the "D" person is active toward tasks, this personality is active toward people. They are charismatic and can be charming and may come across as manipulating other people to get their way. While there is no "I" in team, there is definitely the word, "me", and that is the basis for the "I" personality. It's all about "me." Anyone is welcome to come along on the journey, but just remember who the journey is about. The "I" personality is the life of the party. This person will talk to anyone at the "drop of a hat" and will even drop the hat just to be able to talk. The "I" personality never meets a stranger and you will leave the conversation thinking that you are their new best friend. The Apostle Peter is a biblical example of this personality type.

The classic example of this person is the kid in class who raises their hand to answer a question, but when called on they have no idea of what the question even was. This is the untainted "I" personality. Their personality is energized by other people at whatever cost. This personality seems to get very little accomplished, which is fine with them. They just want and need to be around people. They are not confrontational and are susceptible to peer-pressure. Many times, they will go against their own convictions in order to "go with the crowd." Peer approval is important to them and sought after.

People with high "I" tendencies influence others through talking and activity and tend to be emotional. They are described as convincing, magnetic, political, enthusiastic, persuasive, warm, demonstrative, trusting, and optimistic. For those with low "I" tendencies, they influence more by data and facts, and not with feelings. They are described as reflective, factual, calculating, skeptical, logical, suspicious, matter of fact, pessimistic, and critical. For the high "I," attention to detail and follow through is not important. Their charm and charisma can often lead them to take on many tasks, which may never actually get started— much less completed.

These people can become a strong leader through their natural ability to inspire. They also make great con men. An "I" is very spontaneous and thinks better "on their feet" than with a prepared speech. When leading "I" personalities, remember that recognition and praise are important to these people. Also, remember that when talking to an "I" personality, they are not really listening, but trying to figure out how to get back in control of the conversation. It may not be a conscious thought, but this is how that personality works. Instead of listening, they are thinking about what they want to say next.

Listening skills are NOT in their natural skill set; this needs to become a learned behavior. Leaders may have to repeat themselves often, write it down for them, and then have the "I" state back the task. They will remember every person they meet, but not what the discussion was about. Because of their ability to be flexible and spontaneous, they can quickly turn a situation to their favor and come out of the situation looking very good. They respond to pressure by becoming even more talkative and persuasive. To grow and mature, this person needs to temper inspiration with detail and must learn that others, besides themselves, have goals and influence. The "I" needs to remember: rather than looking inward and at what people can do for them, begin to look at other people and what they can do for others. The "I" personality would benefit from the Apostle Paul in Philippians 2:1-4 (Spirit Filled Life Bible (NKJV), 1991):

> Therefore if there is any consolation in Christ, if any comfort of love, if any fellowship of the Spirit, if any affection and mercy, fulfill my joy by being likeminded, having the same love, being of one accord, of one mind. Let nothing be done through selfish ambition or conceit, but in lowliness of mind let each esteem others better than himself. Let each of you look out not only for his own interests, but also for the interests of others

The "I" person must learn to esteem others even higher. As they invest in relationships that help others, they will find the greatest release for their inspiration and influence. As they grow and mature, they will shift away from what others can do for them and begin to think about what they can do for others. "I's" need to add task completion to their skill set, which will develop them into a strong and accomplished leader. The "I" has a natural

I

Inspiring, Influential, Interesting & Interactive

Active & People-Oriented

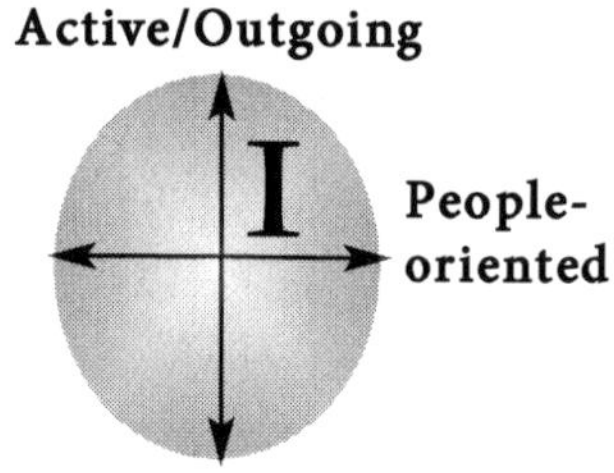

Greatest Strengths:
- Bring a group together
- Flexibility & spontaneity

Greatest Fear:
- Being overlooked

Greatest Challenge:
- Sharing the spotlight with others

Bible Example:
- Peter

Need to focus on:
- Organization
- Time management
- Listening

ability to care for people, but not a natural ability to take care of tasks. Inspiration and influence are two of the most powerful tools available to become a great leader. People skills are their specialty. They have a tremendous ability to draw crowds together and motivate them to a higher purpose.

DISC Types: S—Steady and Stable

The "S" personality is always on everybody's "get-to-know" list. They provide the stability and backbone for any and all groups or organizations. These people hold the group together and are the easiest people to be around. Being the nicest people in the group, they are just enjoyable. They may seem to be quiet and shy at first, but they "warm up" once they get to know you. The Apostle Andrew provides a biblical example of an "S" personality.

While this personality is passive toward people, their value is immeasurable to the group. They may seem to be quiet and shy at first, but they really "warm up" once they get to know you. They will talk very little in the beginning stages of the group; however, once they are comfortable with people, they can talk non-stop. "S" personalities are easy to talk to and comfortable to be around. They want to know "who" is involved prior to committing to a task, project, party, or dinner. These people are the perfect balance to the look-at-me "I" personality because they prefer to talk to people behind the scenes. When the task or group runs into trouble spots, they calm everyone down and keep them focused and working together.

The "S" personality prefers people over tasks, but prefers to work one-on-one or in small groups. Many times the more active personalities, "D" and "I," will take the credit for much of the work done by the "S." However, that is fine with the "S;" they are not interested and would strongly prefer NOT to be in the limelight or get all the attention. Their quiet nature leads them to be thoughtful and intuitive people. People with high "S" traits want a steady pace, security, and do not like sudden changes. High "S" individuals are calm, relaxed, patient, possessive, predictable, deliberate, stable, consistent, and tend to be shy. In contrast, low "S" intensity traits are those who like change and variety. People with low "S" tendencies are described as restless, impatient, demonstrative, eager, or impulsive.

S

STEADY, STABLE & SUPPORTIVE

REFLECTIVE/PASSIVE/RESERVED & PEOPLE-ORIENTED

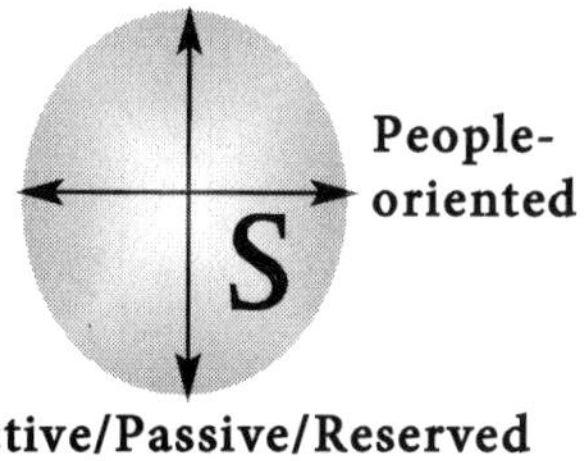

Greatest Strengths:

Backbone of a group
Working behind the scenes

Greatest Fear:

Being alone

Greatest Challenge:

Confrontation

Bible Example:

Andrew

Need to focus on:

Standing up for what they believe
Friendship isn't everything

The "S" personalities are not strong task-oriented people; their strength is in looking out for others. They are much more interested in the general welfare of the people in the group rather than actually getting the work done which becomes the need of this personality. To be successful, it is important for them to acknowledge the task while working to keep the group together. To this personality group, it is all about their relationship with others. A wise leader will recognize this and "task" the "S" to work with the people of the group. Where the "I" is all about "me," the "S" is all about "you."

DISC Types: C—Cautious and Competent

The "C" personality team members are truly the people that get much of the actual work of a task or project done. The "C" personality is initially passive or reserved towards tasks; however, once organized the amount of work accomplished can be staggering. They prefer a checklist of items to be accomplished. The leader of the group may have to help these people with the list, but once it has been developed they will work tirelessly and efficiently in completing the list. The "C" traits demonstrate competence, compliance and caution. The Apostle Thomas exhibits these personality traits.

This is where much of the actual work gets done. While the "S" provides the glue, the "C" provides the substance and task completion for the group. The "C" personalities are not strong in relationships, but they are very strong in task completion. Most significant to the "C" traits is competency. Whereas, the "D" thinks they are always right, the "C" normally is always right. It is best not to disagree or contradict a "C" too quickly because you will most likely be apologizing soon.

"C" types are slow in making a decision, but once the decision is made it is virtually immutable. "C" personalities make great analysts. They will analyze something from every known angle and will even make up angles to study. This gives the appearance of being slow to decide, but to them all the facts are valuable and must be considered prior to making an accurate and lasting conclusion. People with high "C" styles adhere to rules, regulations, and structure. These people are good in quality control and

C

COMPETENT, COMPLIANT & CAUTIOUS

REFLECTIVE/PASSIVE/RESERVED & TASK-ORIENTED

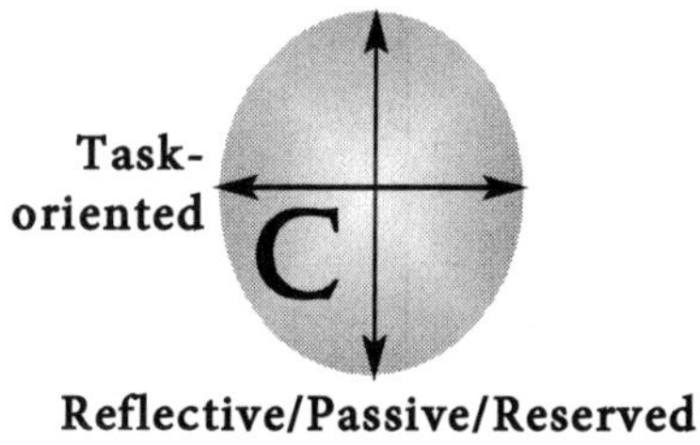

Greatest Strengths:
- Accuracy
- Quality control

Greatest Fear:
- Being wrong

Greatest Challenges:
- Flexibility
- Taking risks

Bible Examples:
- Moses & Thomas

Need to focus on:
- Avoiding perfectionism
- Trust & faith

compliance review. They like to do quality work and do it right the first time.

A "C" personality is known for being compliant which can by definition be seen as obedient, submissive, or yielding; however, this is not the "C" personality. It's important to understand that this personality is compliant, but it's being compliant to their own personal standards. If their standards differ from the company rules, it will be their standards that they follow. The goal for a "C" should be to make God's standards their own. The "C" personality has built-in the ability to follow Shakespeare's admonition: "to thine own self be true"—regardless of circumstance or outside pressure. This is the single person in a jury who votes innocent when everyone else votes guilty; if they change their mind, it will be because they are absolutely convinced that they are wrong—not pressured into it. High "C" people are careful, cautious, exacting, neat, systematic, diplomatic, accurate, and tactful. Those with low "C" scores challenge the rules and want independence and are described as self-willed, stubborn, opinionated, arbitrary, unsystematic, and unconcerned with details.

DISC Style and Conflict

Much like death and taxes, conflict is a guaranteed part of life. It is not a question of IF conflict will come but WHEN. Many times, conflict may be the product of cultural values clashing. Elmer identifies that the Western use of "directness" may be beneficial in Western type cultures; however, in the non-Western cultures that make up the majority of the world, the direct/confrontational approach would be considered rude and immature (Elmer, 1993, p. 48). Global leaders must begin to hear what they are saying and try to understand what is actually being heard when they speak. Global leaders need to develop the personal skills of an active listener. Winston and Patterson defined active listening as the process of hearing the follower's emotions and intent as well as the spoken words (Winston & Patterson, 2006).

According to Stephen Covey, the fifth habit of highly effective people is to seek first to understand, then to be understood; this habit focuses on empathic or active listening which encourages people to listen with the intent of understanding before presenting their own information and opinions (Covey, 1989, p. 239). Active listening will help leaders understand themselves as well as gather information about other cultures. Over 5000 years ago, the great strategist Sun Tzu taught (The Denma Translation Group, 2003):

> If you know the enemy and know yourself, you need not fear the result of a hundred battles. If you know yourself but not the enemy, for every victory gained you will also suffer a defeat. If you know neither the enemy nor yourself, you will succumb in every battle.

Sun Tzu highlights the importance of knowing information about both sides in order to gain an advantage. As leaders practice the art of active listening, both sides gain an advantage.

Conflict has been around since the Garden of Eden, and it continued after the fall of man with Cain and Abel. Gudykunst and Kim conclude that communication is the medium through which conflict is created and managed (Gudykunst & Kim, 2003, p. 296). Conflicts cannot be ignored. They must be resolved. According to Galbraith, organizational structure can generate its own levels of conflict and can easily produce more disagreements as well as confusion (Galbraith J. R., 2000, pp. 71-72). Bass concludes that in organizational life, a typical manager may spend up to 25% of the organization's time dealing with conflicts which can be caused by many factors including organizational structure as well as personality driven conflict (Bass B., 2008, pp. 319-320). Left unresolved, personality conflicts may even lead faithful and diligent workers to leave an organization.

Often, the greatest hindrances to healthy relationships are personality conflicts. Positive individuals, desiring to build good relationships, are often discouraged because of misunderstandings and clashes with others. Personalities and conflict management resolution are designed to discover why people do what they do under pressure and why conflict occurs with others. Success in life principles on how to handle clashes is not always clear. The problem is many people are not aware of their "sensitive spots."

Everyone needs to learn more about avoiding and resolving conflicts. Every personality has its "hot button." but should develop the measure for self-control through understanding others. The following are tendencies of personalities as they relate under pressure (Carbonell, 1993):

"D" Behavior—	**"I" Behavior—**
Under Pressure: Becomes dictatorial, domineering, demanding, angry, intense, foreceful, direct, bossy. **Sources of Irritation:** Weakness, indecisiveness, laziness, Lack of—discipline, plan, purpose, direction, authority, control, challenge. **Needs To:** Back off, seek peace, relax, think before reacting, control self, be—patient, loving, friendly, loyal, kind, sensitive.	**Under Pressure:** Becomes hyper, overly optimistic, immature, emotional, irrational, silly, wordy, selfish. **Sources of Irritation:** Disinterest, slowness, pessimism, details, time restraints, antagonism, doubt, structure, lack of—enthusiasm, team participation. **Needs To:** Listen, count the cost, control emotions, be—humble, strong, disciplined, punctual, careful with words, conscientious.
"C" Behavior—	**"S" Behavior—**
Under Pressure: Becomes moody, critical, contemplative, negative, worrisome. **Sources of Irritation:** Incompetence, disorganization, foolishness, dishonesty, inaccuracy, wastefulness, inconsistency, blind faith, false impressions. **Needs To:** Loosen up, communicate, be—joyful, positive, tolerant, compromising, open, trusting, enthusiastic.	**Under Pressure:** Becomes subservient, insecure, fearful, weak-willed, withdrawn, sympathizer, sucker. **Sources of Irritation:** Pushiness, instability, inflexibility, anger, disloyalty, insensitivity, pride, discrimination, unfairness. **Needs To:** Be—strong, courageous, challenging, aggressive, assertive, confrontational, enthusaiastic, outgoing, expressive, cautious, bold.

Understanding the differences between these styles makes it possible to identify the types of confrontational responses that each of these personality blends may demonstrate and how to respond to each. Most conflict is primarily the result of a miscommunication, frustration, and misunderstanding. Frustration is the product of un-met expectations; we expect people to act in a certain way, but they do not. With an understanding of the four basic personality types, conflict and frustration can be greatly reduced in an organization.

In response to personality-based conflict management and resolution, Carbonell has developed a Resolution Management Promise contract as a means of resolving personality-based organizational conflicts and suggests that organizations include this contract as a signed policy for all employees during their orientation period (Carbonell, 1993, pp. 119-120). This contract is based upon the Biblical principle found in Matthew 18:15-17 of going first to the offended person alone and if that does not work then bring along a neutral individual to help mediate the conflict.

Leading with Style

If motivation represents why we do things, then style represents how we do things. Style can be a noun, verb, adjective or adverb and has the basic definition of a particular manner or technique by which something is done, created, or performed (Merriam-Webster.com, 2011). Replacing the word "something" in this definition with the word "leadership" would produce a definition of leadership style as a particular manner or technique by which leadership is done, created, or performed. Leadership style becomes how that leader accomplishes this definition. The essence of leadership is to get something done. How those things get done can vary from person to person.

With over seven billion people in the world and over seven billion unique plans for their lives, each person must be unique. The Lord does not need copies or duplicates. He creates all people with a unique expression of style in order to fulfill the plan and purpose that He has for their lives. Every one of the unique plans given by the Lord requires a unique expression. God has made leaders the way they are for a purpose and equipped them with a unique style to accomplish their plan and purpose. Many times, leaders will see someone else and want to be like them. The problem with that is the other person has their own assignment. Each person has their own purpose and destiny, so the Lord has given to everyone a different and distinct style to complete His plan and purpose. Since the Lord knew everyone before they were in the womb, their style is one of the first gifts given by Him. He knows the plans that He has for each one and they are good. Therefore, the leadership style that He gives each individual is good because it is needed to complete the plan.

What's Your Style?

There are lengthy commercial surveys available in the marketplace to help identify DISC leadership style and motivation; however, for all practical purposes, your leadership style determination only requires the answer to two questions:

- Outgoing or reserved in a leadership setting?
- Primarily interested in people or tasks?

Once these two questions have been answered, return to the matrix above and plot the answers to the correct quadrant. For example, if the answers were outgoing towards tasks, then quadrant "D" would be the leader and motivational style. This same model can be used to identify the rest of the team's style and motivation. Because each style and motivation is unique, a well-balanced team will have all four motivations represented; for example, the "D" sets the tasks, the "I" keeps the group working together, the "S" provides stability to the group, and the "C" provides a checklist needed to complete the task.

Leadership style and motivation work hand-in-hand as leaders interact with followers. Together, they provide the how and why of leaders' interaction. As leaders work toward understanding these components of leadership, they become better equipped as leaders. The unique expressions of the leadership style and motivation given by the Lord to each individual to complete His plans and purposes are an essential tool for a successful leader and organization.

Transactional and Transformational Personalities

Personalities in society and leadership tend to be described as being either transactional or transformational. Transactional leaders achieve set goals by acting within established procedures and standards. This leader assigns specific, well-defined tasks to subordinates and requires that they fulfill their responsibilities to meet the standards precisely as agreed upon. Transactional leadership emphasizes that the exchange that occurs between the leader and the follower is more directive in nature regarding the requirements and objectives (Bass B., 2008).

Reward and correction methods are based upon the "carrot and stick" approach. Rewards are contingent upon a successful completion of the "transaction". Meeting the objectives typically leads to rewards and reinforcement of the successful performance. The transactional rewards are primarily material (e.g. raise, award or "job security"). Corrective actions are typically more reactive than proactive—the leader monitors the deviations, mistakes and errors in the performance of the subordinates. Failure to reach the objectives will bring disappointment, dissatisfaction, and a psychological (e.g. negative feedback, disapproval, disciplinary actions) or material punishment (Bass B., 2008). Transformational leadership goes beyond just monitoring the performance of the followers and being reactive by providing negative feedback and corrective action when noticing an issue. It also puts a great emphasis on being proactive by establishing long-term goals, facilitating change, seeking continuous improvement, and giving the followers an opportunity to learn from their mistakes.

Unlike transactional leaders, transformational leaders achieve organizational goals by inspiring and motivating followers as well as encouraging their initiatives. Transformational leaders are able to establish a shared vision and sense of purpose among team members. Transformational leaders motivate their followers by raising their concerns from basic needs (e.g. security) to achievement and self-fulfillment; by moving them beyond self-interest to the concerns of the group, project or organization (Burns, 1978). They bring charisma, inspiration, intellectual stimulation, and individualized considerations (Bass B., 2008). Like transactional leadership, contingent rewards are present with transformational leadership and include both psychological and material ones (Bass B., 2008). Transformational leadership however, puts a great emphasis on the psychological rewards with the follower's self-actualization and rising above basic needs. Positive feedback and praise are also examples of psychological rewards. Transformational leadership goes beyond just monitoring the performance of the followers and being reactive (providing negative feedback and corrective action when noticing an issue). It also puts a great emphasis on being proactive, establishing long-term goals, facilitating change, seeking continuous improvement, and giving the followers an opportunity to learn from their mistakes.

Any of the four DISC types of leaders can be transactional or transformational. In some cases, the situation may dictate the leadership style. However, the transformative personality will focus conflict resolution upon two main areas; renewing the mind, which encourages people in conflict to control their personality rather than having their personality control them and mentoring/discipling, which focuses upon people being able to understand the other person's behavior/response before trying to explain their own (Parsons, 2012, p. 92). After all, conflict cannot be ignored, it must be resolved. Developing an understanding and awareness of personality conflicts can be the first step in leaders developing their own personality and conflict management resolution program as well as establishing their transactional/transformational leadership style and understanding all members of their organization.

Chapter 15
Biblical Examples of DISC

Although I am a free man and not anyone's slave, I have made myself a slave to everyone, in order to win more people. To the Jews I became like a Jew, to win Jews; to those under the law, like one under the law—though I myself am not under the law—to win those under the law. To those who are without that law, like one without the law—not being without God's law but within Christ's law—to win those without the law. To the weak I became weak, in order to win the weak. I have become all things to all people, so that I may by every possible means save some. Now I do all this because of the gospel, so I may become a partner in its benefits.
1 Corinthians 9:19-23 (HCSB)

Near the end of the first century, all of the original Apostles were gone—except one. The other eleven have gone on to receive their rewards with the Savior. Martyrdom also claimed the ones that came later such as Paul and Mark. The Apostle John is the last remaining of the original twelve. Why did God choose these men? How did He individually equip them to endure all the adversity—even to the point of death—and continue to build the church?

John remembers when Jerusalem was destroyed in 70 AD all too well. The Roman Empire had taken notice of the Christian Kingdom and decided to obliterate it and kill the last of the original apostles. However, the Apostle John does not die easily and the church only grows more and more. Many accounts of Jesus Christ have circulated throughout the church. Some have been accurate, but not all. Not wanting to reproduce the writings of others, John surveys the church and prepares to bring forth a book directed by the

Holy Spirit filled with new revelations. The year is approximately 90 AD, and the beloved disciple John begins to pen his own gospel (Hayford, 1995). While this fourth gospel does not explicitly identify its author, Irenaeus, the Bishop of Lyons, identified the author as the Apostle John; hence, church tradition holds that this Gospel of John was indeed written by the Apostle John in the city of Ephesus.

As he writes, John begins to think back to his brothers in the faith and surveys what an unlikely mix of characters were used by the Lord to establish His church. Peter had a big smile on his face and was always good for a laugh. He. He had a way of making people feel like they were his best friend. John also thinks of Peter's brother, Andrew. So unlike his brother, Andrew was quiet and shy, but steady and stable. Where Peter would fall apart, Andrew would always keep things together. However, once Andrew got to know you, he would really warm up and talk and laugh as much as Peter. Peter was great in a crowd, but Andrew could always be seen working one-on-one ministering to people individually.

John begins to miss them all, even Thomas. He recalls how Thomas always got a bad rap for the time he questioned Jesus. John understands that Thomas' personality needs concrete proof in order to believe, and it didn't seem to bother Jesus because He never rebuked or scolded Thomas concerning his questions. However, once converted, he was committed to the cause. Thomas was more like Paul than the other apostles in that once he set his mind and heart on something, he was unstoppable.

John wonders about the diverse group of people that came together to be called the Apostles of the Lamb. Why were they all so different? What made each one so unique? Their personalities were completely different, but uniquely suited for the plan and purpose which the Lord had for each of them individually and for the group as a whole. John recalls that when he first saw Paul, who was known then as Saul of Tarsus, at the Sanhedrin council in Jerusalem there was nobody else like him. He was brash, arrogant, and always on the go doing something. It seemed as if Saul of Tarsus might be able to single-handedly destroy the Good News by arresting and persecuting the entire church.

Paul: Direct and Demanding

> So, being sent out by the Holy Spirit, they [Paul and Barnabas] went down to Seleucia, and from there they sailed to Cyprus. And when they arrived in Salamis, they preached the word of God in the synagogues of the Jews. (Acts 13:4-5: NKJV).

After Paul's conversion, he spread the gospel of Jesus across more nations than the rest of them combined. Saul of Tarsus is first introduced to Bible readers in Acts 7:58 at the stoning of the first Christian martyr, Stephen. Saul is identified as a young man in verse 58. History records that Saul was born between 10-15 A.D. (Ludwig, 1983, p. 172). This would put Saul in his late teens to early twenties. Saul probably traveled to Jerusalem presumably at the age of 13 to study under the renowned Rabban Gamaliel who was the grandson of one of the most important figures in Jewish history, Hillel (Ludwig, 1983, p. 177).

Saul would have been a member of the Sanhedrin, which was the Jewish ruling assembly at the time. He was an ambitious man who studied under the best and achieved success early and often. After the stoning of Stephen, Saul goes on a one-man crusade to eradicate the religion of Jesus Christ (Halley, 1980, p. 567). Saul begins the first persecution of the church in Acts chapters 8 and 9. In Acts 9:1, Saul is "breathing threats and murder against the Disciples of Christ" (NKJV). At this point, Saul can be identified as an active, task-oriented leader with the goal of removing the Christian church from the face of the earth. However, on his way to Damascus, he has an encounter that will change his life and future, forever. In Acts 9:3-6, Saul encounters the same Jesus that he was trying to eliminate. Saul's destiny changes that day, but not his leadership style. After his conversion and subsequent healing at the hands of Ananias, Saul immediately begins to preach Jesus Christ in the synagogues of Damascus. After this conversion, he begins to actively spread the gospel around the known world. Saul of Tarsus becomes the Apostle Paul who traveled to more countries and more diverse people on foot than many do today with all the transportation means available. Paul was determined to fulfill the Great Commission of going into the entire world and making Christian disciples all on his own. Saul of Tarsus was direct, demanding, decisive, and doing all the wrong things. When he was converted to Christianity, his leadership style did not change, only his purpose. The Apostle Paul was direct, demanding, decisive, and doing the unique plan and purpose that he was called to complete. Paul spends the next 30 years of his life actively pursuing the task of expanding the Kingdom of God and is eventually beheaded by Nero (Elwell & Yarbrough, 1998). His leadership style was uniquely suited for the plan and purpose that God called him to complete.

According to Bass, task-oriented leaders like Paul are identified as achievement oriented, production oriented, production emphasizing, goal achieving, work facilitative, goal emphasizing, performance planning and performance pressuring (Bass B., 2008, p. 498). Yukl proposes five purposes of task-oriented leader behavior (Yukl, 2009):

- To propose an objective, introduce a procedure, present an agenda, and redirect attention to the task.
- To stimulate communication, seek specific information, or encourage the introduction of new ideas.
- To clarify communication, reduce confusion, ask for interpretations, and show how different ideas are related.
- To summarize accomplishments, to review or ask for reviews.
- To test for consensus about objectives, interpretations, evaluations, and readiness for decisions

Peter: Inspiring and Influential

> But Peter, standing up with the eleven, raised his voice and said to them, "Men of Judea and all who dwell in Jerusalem, let this be known to you, and heed my words. For these are not drunk, as you suppose, since it is only the third hour of the day. But this is what was spoken by the prophet Joel.
> (Acts 2:14-16 NKJV).

On the Day of Pentecost, Peter was the one who stood up and proclaimed the word of the Lord about the gift of the Holy Spirit. When Peter was active, he was always active towards people — not tasks. Peter is first introduced to Bible readers in Matthew 4:18 where, along with his brother

Andrew, he is identified as being a fisherman. Peter is from Bethsaida, which means house of fishing (Strong, 1981) and is located along the coast of Galilee. He has a vastly different upbringing than Saul of Tarsus. Peter has a different leadership style and a different purpose in the Kingdom. Peter alone is called out of the boat to walk on the water in Matthew 14:27-30. Peter is the one who speaks without thinking and actually rebukes Jesus in Matthew 16:22 when Jesus begins to reveal the plan of God that He has to come to fulfill. Peter is the one who denied Jesus three times. He openly expressed his thoughts and was usually the first disciple to speak in any given situation. On the Day of Pentecost, Peter is emboldened by the infilling of the Holy Spirit and preaches the first sermon to the crowds where over 3000 people were born again (Acts 2:14-41). Even though John is with Peter in Acts chapter three, it is Peter who responds to the man begging for alms. In Acts 3:6, Peter said to him, "Silver and gold I do not have, but what I do have I give you: In the name of Jesus Christ of Nazareth, rise up and walk" (Spirit Filled Life Bible (NKJV), 1991). This is the first recorded miracle performed by the any of the apostles. Peter goes on to preach in Solomon's Portico and is subsequently arrested.

When testifying to the Sanhedrin, Peter is the one who boldly proclaims that Jesus has been raised from the dead and that salvation is only available through Him (Acts 4:1-12). In Acts 5:29, Peter is the one identified in Scripture as becoming the spokesman for the group. While Scripture does not explicitly record that Saul of Tarsus was present, he was a member of the Sanhedrin in Jerusalem and should have had full knowledge of the events of the day. Jesus was also brought to this same Sanhedrin in Matthew 26:57-68, which suggests that it is possible that Saul of Tarsus was present during the "trial" and execution of Jesus. Even Paul's teacher, Rabban Gamaliel, had begun to be swayed by persuasive Peter and the other apostles. This may be why such a strong response was elicited from Saul against the Christian faith prior to his conversion. Gamaliel's story is recorded in Acts 5:33-39 (HCSB, 2010):

> When they heard this, they were enraged and wanted to kill them. A Pharisee named Gamaliel, a teacher of the law who was respected by all the people, stood up in the Sanhedrin and

> ordered the men to be taken outside for a little while. He said to them, "Men of Israel, be careful about what you're going to do to these men. Not long ago Theudas rose up, claiming to be somebody, and a group of about 400 men rallied to him. He was killed, and all his partisans were dispersed and came to nothing. After this man, Judas the Galilean rose up in the days of the census and attracted a following. That man also perished, and all his partisans were scattered. And now, I tell you, stay away from these men and leave them alone. For if this plan or this work is of men, it will be overthrown; but if it is of God, you will not be able to overthrow them. You may even be found fighting against God." So they were persuaded by him.

Peter becomes the first apostle to reach out to the Gentiles after the vision on the rooftop in Joppa that resulted in his visit to Cornelius, a centurion of the Italian Regiment in Acts chapter 10. However, this is not Peter's first encounter with a Roman soldier. He was in the Garden of Gethsemane when Judas came with troops to arrest Jesus. In the garden, Peter used a sword to cut off the ear of Malchus. However, he responds very differently to Cornelius by preaching the Gospel of Jesus to him and his household. Scripture records in Acts 10:44-45 (Spirit Filled Life Bible (NKJV), 1991):

> While Peter was still speaking these words, the Holy Spirit fell upon all those who heard the word. And those of the circumcision who believed were astonished, as many as came with Peter, because the gift of the Holy Spirit had been poured out on the Gentiles also.

Once again, it is Peter who responds to the people and the Holy Spirit is poured out to the Gentiles. He was also in Antioch with Paul ministering to the Gentiles until certain Jewish leaders came to the area. Being a leader that is motivated to please people, Peter withdrew from the Gentiles and was sharply rebuked by Paul in Galatians 2:11-14 (HCSB, 2010):

> But when Cephas came to Antioch, I opposed him to his face because he stood condemned. For he regularly ate with the

> Gentiles before certain men came from James. However, when they came, he withdrew and separated himself, because he feared those from the circumcision party. Then the rest of the Jews joined his hypocrisy, so that even Barnabas was carried away by their hypocrisy. But when I saw that they were deviating from the truth of the gospel, I told Cephas in front of everyone, "If you, who are a Jew, live like a Gentile and not like a Jew, how can you compel Gentiles to live like Jews?"

Peter was a leader who was impulsive yet warm, friendly, outspoken, and active towards people. He continues to preach the gospel of Jesus Christ for about 30 years and is eventually crucified by Nero (Elwell & Yarbrough, 1998).

Where Paul was more task-oriented, Peter is more relations-oriented and concerned with what people think about him. Peter follows what Yukl describes as a relations-oriented leadership style that expresses concern for people and attempts to reduce emotional conflict by harmonizing relations among others (Yukl, 2009). Peter presents a personality style that is inspiring, influencing, impressing, inducing, and active towards people. His basic motivation is recognition and approval.

The Apostle Andrew: Steady and Stable

"He [Andrew] first found his own brother Simon,
and said to him, 'We have found the Messiah.'"
(John 1:41: NKJV)

The "S" personality influences one-on-one to bring people together and works more efficiently and effectively behind the scenes. The Apostle Andrew is a perfect example as recorded in John 1:29-42 (Spirit Filled Life Bible (NKJV), 1991):

> The next day John saw Jesus coming toward him and said, "Here is the Lamb of God, who takes away the sin of the world! This is the One I told you about: 'After me comes a

> man who has surpassed me, because He existed before me.' I didn't know Him, but I came baptizing with water so He might be revealed to Israel." And John testified, "I watched the Spirit descending from heaven like a dove, and He rested on Him. I didn't know Him, but He who sent me to baptize with water told me, 'The One you see the Spirit descending and resting on—He is the One who baptizes with the Holy Spirit.' I have seen and testified that He is the Son of God!" Again, the next day, John stood with two of his disciples. And looking at Jesus as He walked, he said, "Behold the Lamb of God!" The two disciples heard him speak, and they followed Jesus. Then Jesus turned, and seeing them following, said to them, "What do you seek?" They said to Him, "Rabbi" (which is to say, when translated, Teacher), "where are You staying?" He said to them, "Come and see." They came and saw where He was staying, and remained with Him that day (now it was about the tenth hour). One of the two who heard John speak, and followed Him, was Andrew, Simon Peter's brother. He first found his own brother Simon, and said to him, "We have found the Messiah" (which is translated, the Christ). And he brought him to Jesus

The New Testament states that Peter had a brother named Andrew. The name "Andrew" means manly and brave with valor. Both he and Peter were fishermen by trade; hence, Jesus called them to be His disciples by saying that He will make them "fishers of men." At the beginning of Jesus' public life, these brothers lived together in the same house in Capernaum. Mark 1:29 reads, "Now as soon as they had come out of the synagogue, they entered the house of Simon and Andrew, with James and John." As brothers tend to be, the men were very different. Where Peter was loud, boisterous, and the life of the party as the "I" personality, Andrew was more quiet, steady, stable, and secure. Andrew was more of an "S" personality. The Gospel of John states that Andrew was a disciple of John the Baptist, whose testimony first led him to follow Jesus. Andrew preferred a more one-on-one encounter. He at once recognized Jesus as the Messiah, and he hastened to introduce him to his brother, Peter. Andrew wasn't the one chosen to preach to the multitudes, but God used his personality to minister to one person at a time. Mother Teresa once said, "Help one person at a time and always start with the person nearest you." This adage is the mantra for the "S" personality.

As noted above on the occasion of the miraculous feeding of the five thousand, it was Andrew who knew about the lone boy in the crowd and said to Jesus in Acts 6:9-6 that, "There is a boy here who has five barley loaves and two fishes: but what are these among so many?" While quiet by nature, Andrew was loyal and a close member of Jesus' inner council of friends. For example, a few days before Jesus' death, certain Greeks asked Philip if they might see Jesus; Philip referred the matter to Andrew as to one of greater clout. Andrew brought stability and authority to the group.

In the Gospels, Andrew is referred to as being present for some important occasions as one of the disciples closely attached to Jesus. Andrew preferred small groups and left the larger audiences to Peter. He worked better in the background and, consequently, not much more information is mentioned about him in the Scriptures. From what we generally know of the Apostles, we can extrapolate the details. As one of the Twelve, Andrew was allowed into Jesus' inner-circle; he was present at the Last Supper; beheld the risen Lord; witnessed the Ascension; shared in the graces and gifts of the first Pentecost; and helped, amid threats and persecution, to establish the gospel in Palestine and other areas. According to church history and tradition, he is considered the founder and first bishop of the Church of Byzantium (later Constantinople) in AD 38. Andrew, therefore, sows the first seeds into the area that Constantine will later make the seat of Christianity in the Roman Empire.

Early church leaders such as Eusebius and Origen state that Andrew preached in Asia Minor and in Scythia, along the Black Sea as far as the cities of Volga and Kiev. Christian history in the Ukraine holds that the Apostle Andrew is said to have preached on the southern borders of modern-day Ukraine, along the Black Sea. Legend has it that he travelled up the Dnieper River and reached the future location of Kiev, where he erected a cross on the site where the St. Andrew's Church of Kiev currently stands, and he prophesied the foundation of a great Christian city. Like his brother Peter, Andrew traveled and ministered for about 30 years and is martyred by crucifixion at the city of Patras in Greece.

Church tradition describes Andrew as bound, not nailed, to a Latin cross of the kind on which Jesus is said to have been crucified. However, because he deemed himself unworthy to be crucified in the same manner as the Lord Jesus, Andrew requested to be crucified on a cross of the form called Crux decussata (X-shaped cross) now commonly known as a "Saint Andrew's Cross." The Apostle Andrew did not die right away, but instead he was left to suffer for two days. True to his nature and his personality, church tradition records that he continued to preach the gospel of Jesus Christ bound to the cross until he finally died.

Tradition states that his martyrdom took place during the reign of Nero on November 30, AD 60, and both the Latin and Greek churches keep that day as his feast. Because of his travels, Andrew became the patron saint of Scotland, Ukraine, Russia, Romania, Patras in Greece, Amalfi in Italy, Luqa in Malta (where Paul was previously shipwrecked), and Esgueira in Portugal. He was also the patron saint of Prussia. While quiet and steady in his personality, he fulfilled his plan and purpose of expanding the Kingdom of God and preaching the gospel throughout many countries. Church tradition places the Apostle Andrews' remains in the Cathedral of Amalfi in Italy.

The Apostle Thomas: Cautious & Competent

> And after eight days His disciples were again inside, and Thomas with them. Jesus came, the doors being shut, and stood in the midst, and said, "Peace to you!" Then He said to Thomas, "Reach your finger here, and look at My hands; and reach your hand here, and put it into My side. Do not be unbelieving, but believing." And Thomas answered and said to Him, "My Lord and my God!" (John 20:26-28: NKJV).

Thomas the Apostle, or Didymus (meaning "Twin") was also one of the twelve Apostles of Jesus. Thomas was born in or near Galilee. Through the Scripture, we see that he represents a classic "C" personality. However, Thomas gets a bad rap for being called the Doubting Apostle. Even today, people who are skeptical are called a "Doubting Thomas." In Thomas' best known appearance in the New Testament, he doubts the resurrection of

Jesus and demands to touch Jesus' wounds before being convinced. It is very important to note that Jesus did NOT correct or chastise Thomas for wanting this proof; He simply said, "Touch and feel." However, upon seeing and touching the wounds of Jesus he boldly proclaims, "My Lord and my God."

Thomas was not with them when Jesus appeared the first time in the Upper Room. The other disciples therefore said to him in John 20:24-29 (Spirit Filled Life Bible (NKJV), 1991):

> "We have seen the Lord." So he said to them, "Unless I see in His hands the print of the nails, and put my finger into the print of the nails, and put my hand into His side, I will not believe." And after eight days His disciples were again inside, and Thomas with them. Jesus came, the doors being shut, and stood in the midst, and said, "Peace to you!" Then He said to Thomas, "Reach your finger here, and look at My hands; and reach your hand here, and put it into My side. Do not be unbelieving, but believing." And Thomas answered and said to Him, "My Lord and my God!" Jesus said to him, "Thomas, because you have seen Me, you have believed. Blessed are those who have not seen and yet have believed."

Jesus knew that Thomas' cautious personality required concrete proof and evidence of what had transpired. He also knew that once Thomas had the proof or evidence he needed, he would serve Him without hesitancy for the duration of his life. A "C" personality has a natural desire to analyze and question everything BEFORE making a decision. This is something that the "D" and "I" personalities need desperately to learn. Additionally, once a "C's" mind in convinced, the decision becomes immutable or unchangeable. The decision becomes written in stone, which is demonstrated by Thomas' response to the concrete proof and evidence that Jesus provided: "My Lord and my God." At that point, Thomas was fully persuaded and fully devoted to serve Jesus. Thomas also spoke up when Lazarus died and the apostles didn't want to go back to Judea, where Jesus' fellow Jews had attempted to stone Him to death. However, Thomas is fully convinced and says bravely in John 11:16, "Let us also go, that we may die with him." This personality is not known to be optimistic. As a typical "C" personality, Thomas always has questions to ask as in John 14:1-6 (Spirit Filled Life Bible (NKJV), 1991).

> "Let not your heart be troubled; you believe in God, believe also in Me. In My Father's house are many mansions; if it were not so, I would have told you. I go to prepare a place for you. And if I go and prepare a place for you, I will come again and receive you to Myself; that where I am, there you may be also. And where I go you know, and the way you know." Thomas said to Him, "Lord, we do not know where You are going, and how can we know the way?" Jesus said to him, "I am the way, the truth, and the life. No one comes to the Father except
> through Me.

Thomas can be seen as having a competent, compliant, and cautious personality as we read what he said and did as told in the Bible accounts. However, God used Thomas as perhaps the only original Apostle who went outside the Roman Empire to preach the gospel of Jesus Christ. Once convinced of the resurrection, Thomas was unstoppable. He never wavered from his purpose, even to the point of death. He is also believed to have covered the largest area during the time of his ministry, which includes modern Persia and India. The Apostle Thomas is traditionally believed to have sailed to India in 52 AD to spread the Christian faith in Kerala, India. He is supposed to have landed at the ancient port of Muziris, which became extinct in 1341 AD due to a massive flood which realigned the coasts near Kodungalloor. He then went to Palayoor (near present day Guruvayoor), which was a Hindu priestly community at that time. He left Palayoor in AD 52 for the southern part of what is now the Kerala State.

According to church tradition, Thomas was at first reluctant to accept this mission, but the Lord appeared to him in a night vision and said, "Fear not, Thomas. Go away to India and proclaim the Word, for my grace shall be with you." This response is classic for his "C" personality; he resisted at first and Jesus had to appear to him and instruct him—not rebuke him or correct him, but instruct him. Not being active toward tasks, Thomas again required specific instruction, which is provided by the Lord without question or hesitation. Thomas evangelized throughout India and then crossed to the southeast coast of India where, after carrying out a second mission, he died near Madras. The tradition among Christians in India is that Thomas was speared to death around AD 53. He is often pictured holding a spear.

Like all Christian believers, the Apostles of the Lord Jesus Christ were called for a specific purpose. The first tool given to each of them to assist in the fulfillment of that purpose was their personality. The characteristics and traits of those personalities can be seen throughout their lives.

Chapter 16
Book Industry Innovation

"The key question isn't "What fosters creativity?" But it is why in God's name isn't everyone creative? Where was the human potential lost? How was it crippled? I think therefore a good question might be not why do people create? But why do people not create or innovate? We have got to abandon that sense of amazement in the face of creativity, as if it were a miracle if anybody created anything."
—Abraham Maslow

"The world is but a canvas to the imagination."
—Henry David Thoreau

As emerging innovative leaders work to understand and develop the common core competencies, industry examples can also provide valuable insight into the innovative process. For example, the book industry has been hard-hit in the current economic times. Change is becoming the catalyst to produce new ways of doing business. The writing down of information has its foundation in the beginning of recorded history. From cave walls to clay tablets and from papyrus to paper, the writing of information has undergone many changes over the years. Innovation can be identified as the creative key for changes over time in this industry. As previously stated, innovation has been defined as the intentional development of a specific product, service, idea, environment, or process for the generation of value (Oster, 2011, p. 3). Value and relevance are key words for the continual evolution of the book industry. Publisher's Weekly reports that the number of publishers are declining and many bookstores are closing (Raugust, 2011). While the numbers of publishers are declining, the actual number of books in print had a modest 5% increase in 2010 according to Bowkers, the authoritative source for book publishers and books in print, with an estimated 316,480 books printed (Bowkers, 2011). However, change is once again on the horizon.

Utterback would categorize the book industry as waves of technological change with each change reflecting the fundamental objective but each change also represents a different way of achieving it (Utterback, 1996, pp. 18-19). Again, one of the oldest books ever written is ***The Art of War,*** which is a 7000 word "book" originally written on bamboo strips around 500 B.C. by the master strategist Sun Tzu (Michaelson, 2001). Stones could be the most ancient form of writing, but wood would be the first medium to take the guise of a book. From wood to paper to digital ink, books have survived over the years as the primary medium of communication (Encyclopedia Britannica, 2013).

Creativity

Innovation and creativity are closely linked. To release creativity requires seeing something different than everyone else. Albert Szent-Györgyi, a Hungarian-born biochemist who won the Nobel Prize in 1937, states that creativity and discovery consist of seeing what everybody has seen and thinking what nobody has thought (Szent-Gyorgyi, 1962). According to Oster, creativity requires a careful tending process, and everyone must be absolutely sure that wild and unusual ideas are welcomed as well as ensuring that any impediments to creativity are removed (Oster, 2011).

Perhaps the greatest challenge to releasing creativity is the stifling of the creative process that is required to think strategically. Businesses where creativity is not valued and nurtured will struggle to compete with more visionary enterprises because strategic leadership requires creativity in order to produce effective results (Strategic Direction, 2008). Cooper contends that creativity plays a vital role in the strategic thinking process in order to produce a sustained competitive advantage but also admits that many organizations actually discourage the freedom of practicing creativity (Cooper, 1998). Creative thinkers and innovators never seem to be corporate insiders much less those on the organizational fast track, and many times they need organizational cover from corporate fire since they do everything possible to escape the shackles of precedent, tradition, and orthodoxy (Oster, 2011).

Book Industry Innovation

According to Gryskiewicz, creativity and innovation have been found to be the cornerstone of healthy organizations that are ready for reinventing themselves, and organizations accomplish this by being relevant to changing markets as well as the use of new technology (Gryskiewicz, 1999, p. 1). Clay tablets were used in Mesopotamia in the 3rd millennium BC. The calamus, an instrument in the form of a triangle, was used to make characters in moist clay. The tablets were fired to dry them out. At Nineveh, 22,000 tablets were found, dating from the 7th century BC; this was the archive and library of the kings of Assyria, who had workshops of copyists and conservationists at their disposal. This presupposes a degree of organization with respect to books, consideration given to conservation, classification, etc. Tablets were used right up until the 19th century in various parts of the world, including Germany, Chile, and the Saharan Desert (Encyclopedia Britannica, 2013). Clay tablets eventually gave way to the use of papyrus.

After extracting the marrow from the papyrus stems, a series of steps (humidification, pressing, drying, gluing, and cutting), produced media of variable quality, the best being used for sacred writing. In Ancient Egypt, papyrus may have been used for writing as early as the First Dynasty, but the first evidence is from the account books of King Neferirkare Kakai of the Fifth Dynasty (Avrin, 1991, p. 83). A calamus made from the stem of a reed sharpened to a point, or bird feathers were used for writing. The script of Egyptian scribes was called hieratic or sacredotal writing; it is not hieroglyphic, but a simplified form more adapted to manuscript writing (hieroglyphs usually being engraved or painted). Papyrus evolves into paper and remains the mainstay of books for centuries. However, innovation and creativity were not done with the book industry. The digital age dawns and books begin to embrace a digital format.

The Digital Age

According to a Strategic Study for the Book Publishing Industry in Ontario, forecasters do not see a collapse of physical books as a product, or of book publishing as an industry; however, it will become increasingly difficult to be competitive without adopting appropriate digital print processes, including digital distribution of content apart from the physical book (Castledale Inc, 2008). Offset printing has long been the printing method of choice for physical books. However, this process is slow, expensive, and difficult to change.

The advent of the digital press provides publishers with many more options. The concept is simple. Books are printed after they are ordered rather than before. This removes the need for pre-purchase cost of printing and warehouse storage space and fees. Changes or corrections to the book are quickly and inexpensively accomplished. Digital printing is also known as print-on-demand or POD printing. However, the POD industry is growing and maturing as well as addressing most of the quality issues of the past.

Publishers are also using this print option to keep titles in print longer, especially those selling less than 1,000 copies a year. The POD leader in the US, Lightning Source, now manufactures more than 1.3 million books per month and a few larger publishers in the US have purchased POD systems, which will print titles in their warehouse, one at a time, as they are sold (Thornton, 2008). This technology will only become more affordable in the next few years, allowing medium and smaller publishers to acquire POD systems or access to POD systems. This trend is also changing author agreements as "in print" and "out of print" definitions change.

Electronic Books Abound

According to the New York Times, eBooks and eReaders are upending the way books are published, sold, bought, and read as well as identifying that Barnes & Noble may be putting the future of the company in the hands of its eBook reader, the Nook (Bosman, 2012). With the new iPad, Apple is pushing their tablet deeper into the eBook race along with the Amazon

Kindle. Apple has sold nearly 40 million iPads since its debut in 2010 (Pepitone, 2011). While the iPad is not primarily an eBook Reader, Apple has its own eBook publishing standards that many publishers already use.

However, the Kindle and Nook are primarily eBook readers and the Kindle Fire, which is also a tablet, is reaching 5 million in sales (Pepitone, 2011). Barnes & Noble promotes that the Nook has over 2 million books available (Barnes & Noble, 2011). The Amazon Kindle store reports that 2,270,077 eBooks are available as of 11 October 2013 (Amazon, 2013). Book Business reported on an article written by Albert Greco of the Institute for Publishing Research that sales of print titles will drop from $18 billion in 2008 to $13.9 billion in 2015, and his projections show that e-book sales should increase to $3.6 billion by 2015 from $78 million in 2008 (Greco, 2011).

Innovation Forward

While format has changed over the years from writing on bamboo strips to a digital e-book, content still rules the publishing realm. Regardless of the format of a book, content is still the primary reason for consumers to purchase one. A Gallup poll identified that the primary reason consumers buy a book is for the subject (Woll, 2002). One analysis identifies that bookstores may not be the best place to sell a book due to the competition of other books available and concludes that placing the book in the proper market would be more effective (Bolme, 2006). Hence, even the placement and location to purchase the book has changed over time. Whereas most people might expect that the top reasons to buy books are book covers, marketing, price, reviews, etc., the 1996 Consumer Research Study on Book Publishing reports that the number one reason that consumers purchase a book is the subject of the book (American Booksellers Association, 1996).

Innovations are not unique to the book publishing business as they are sweeping across most industries. In a time of unpredictability, innovation opens the doors to new opportunities for those that are prepared. Working to develop these common core competencies will help emerging innovative leaders be prepared to step-up with new ideas for old systems.

Chapter 17
The Greatest Innovator of All Time

"Therefore, brethren, having boldness to enter the Holiest by the blood of Jesus, by a new and living way which He consecrated for us, through the veil, that is, His flesh, and having a High Priest over the house of God"
Hebrews 10:19-21 (NKJV)

"Therefore, if anyone is in Christ, he is a new creation; old things have passed away; behold, all things have become new"
2 Corinthians 5:17 (NKJV)

Innovation is not a new concept, and history records many great innovators. However, one innovator stands head-and-shoulders above all the rest combined. The greatest innovator of all time is Jesus the Messiah. Jesus was at the right place at the right time to change the course of all mankind—that is innovation. Timing is critical to the concept of innovative leadership. According to Rausch, timing and availability of information are key guidelines that must be considered before leaders should make any significant decisions (Rausch, 1996). When Jesus was born into the family of Joseph and Mary, the timing seemed to be out of synchronization. Not only was the inn full, the Son of God was born in a cave that was commonly used for animals, and shepherds were given the announcement of the birth of the new king rather than the leaders in the current realm (Elwell & Yarbrough, 1998).

However, the creator of the universe had a plan, and the mystery of the ages had begun in the little town of Bethlehem. From an exegetical point-of-view, the social and cultural texture analysis from the Socio-Rhetorical Criticism Model on Matthew 28:1-20 can be used to identify the strategic intent and plans of the early Jesus movement as a countercultural force in the Second Temple Period as well as the implications that this level of strategic and innovative planning holds for contemporary organizations today.

The Second Temple

The Second Temple Period is commonly understood to be the period of time that the second temple existed from its rebuilding around 530 BC to its destruction by the Romans in 70 AD (Sanders J. T., 2001). Wright contends that during this 600 year period of history the Jewish people began looking for the return of a King that would bring peace to the land of Israel which had survived the Babylonian captivity and the rule of the Persians, Greeks, Syrians and finally the Romans (Wright, 1998). In the strategic plan of God the seeds had been sown for a new king and the Jewish people were looking for their king to return at any moment. Into that backdrop, God sends His Son to be born into the earth at the right time with the right message.

God has a time and purpose for all things, including a unique plan to announce His new kingdom and to prepare the way for Jesus. After 400 years of prophetic silence, a prophet, John the Baptist, is heard in the wilderness proclaiming for all to repent because the kingdom of heaven has come near (HCSB, 2010). According to Hayford, the New Testament records 137 references to the "kingdom" and over 100 of these are used during Jesus' time (Spirit Filled Life Bible (NKJV), 1991, p. 1407). Similar to the Essene community of the day, John the Baptist arrives in a camel-hair garment that is still worn by some Arab nomadic tribes (Freeman, 1972). Like the Essenes, John is viewed as a counter-temple movement by preaching in the wilderness about the advent of a new kingdom (Wright, 1998). From the social and cultural texture analysis, Robbins would call the Essenes introversionists who viewed the world as evil and withdrew from it (Robbins, 1996). While most Essenes prefer to stay isolated from the world, John the Baptist had a greater role to play. According to Wright,

John the Baptist is re-enacting the exodus of Israel from Egypt by baptizing his followers in the Jordan River in the wilderness and preparing the people for a new kingdom and a new kingdom message (Wright, 1998). It is time for the plan of the ages to unfold.

From John the Baptist to Jesus

In Matthew 3:13, Jesus travels the 70 miles from Galilee to the Jordan to be baptized by John. France contends that by first identifying with John's proclamation Jesus lays the foundation for his own mission to take on where John is leaving off, and He is identified with all those who by accepting John's baptism have declared it is time for a new beginning with God (France, 2007). Demonstrating leadership succession, Jesus connected with John the Baptist and endorsed his message of repentance because entrance into this new kingdom would not be made by Roman hands. Wright concludes that Jesus embarked on a public career of kingdom-initiation through His connection to John the Baptist and further emphasizes that Jesus was a prophet of the kingdom, first enacting and then explaining that kingdom (Wright, 1999).

In Mark 1:15, Jesus moves away from the introversionist response of the Essenes to the conversionist response by declaring that the Kingdom of God is available to those that repent and believe (Robbins, 1996). Wright contends that the Essenes, John the Baptist and Jesus all had one thing in common; they were all considered a counter-temple movement (Wright, 1998). The Essenes separated themselves from all others, and would not allow anyone with a sickness or disease to become a part of their group. John the Baptist was primarily in one area baptizing and preaching.

However, Jesus went out among the people in the local villages and demonstrated the power of God through healings, miracles, signs and wonders. Wright believes that Jesus was emphasizing that the kingdom was at hand and all are invited to join (Wright, 1999). This type of counter-culture teaching of another kingdom caught the attention of Rome and the counter-temple emphasis of Jesus going into the local villages caught the attention of the religious rulers. Conflict was inevitable.

Matthew 28 and the Kingdom Message

The Kingdom message that Jesus of Nazareth had been teaching comes to a climax in Matthew 28. Rome and the religious leaders ended up working together to remove this counter-cultural and counter-temple movement. The Roman answer to all revolutionary movements was the same: an extremely painful death and utter humiliation through a crucifixion. Horsley and Silberman contend that there was no question or mystery about the brutality of Roman crucifixion because it was the most painful, humiliating, and public display of death and dishonor imaginable (Horsley & Silberman, 2002). While His death on the cross might have been seen as an end to His Kingdom message, the end of one chapter is only the beginning of another, and the exegetical analysis of Matthew 28 confirms this for the Kingdom message.

DeSilva identifies that Matthew probably wrote his gospel after Mark's gospel was written and retains many of the traditions about Jesus; however, Matthew presents a much different picture of Jesus by focusing on Him being the interpreter of the Torah (DeSilva, 2004). Hayford states that Matthew's gospel would have been written between 50-65 AD with the later date being more common because of the noted tension between Jew and Gentile with Judaism and Christianity overlapping in his gospel; Hayford also identifies that Matthew's purpose in his gospel was to proclaim that when the King is present, God's kingdom has come and Jesus is that King (Hayford, 1995).

Matthew 28 can be analyzed with the social and cultural texture analysis identified by Robbins. Social and cultural texture is one of the five textures analyzed using Robbins' Social-Rhetorical Interpretation model. The social and cultural texture of a given text concerns the nature of the text as a part of a society and culture; this texture emerges from insight into how the text views the world through specific social topics, how it shares cultural attitudes and norms through common social and cultural topics, and how it reveals the dominant cultural system (Robbins, 1996).

France divides Matthew 28 into the following three sections (France, 2007):

- The Empty Tomb (Matthew 28:1-10)
- The Priest's Cover-up (Matthew 28:11-15)
- The Messianic Mission (Matthew 28:16-20)

The Empty Tomb (Matthew 28:1-10)

Matthew starts chapter 28 after the actual resurrection with two women, Mary Magdalene and the other Mary, headed to the tomb of Jesus. Two unique groups are identified in this section: the women who discover the empty tomb and the guards who are guarding a tomb that is not supposed to be empty. This section contains a thaumaturgical discourse which focuses on relief from an individual or group's present and specific ills through a special dispensation of the divine (Robbins, 1996). Presumably to mourn, the women head to the tomb only to discover an angel telling them that Jesus is alive. After viewing the empty tomb, they leave quickly to tell the others and are actually met by their risen Lord. Their relief can be noted by their response of holding His feet and worshipping. This section also contains a countercultural rhetoric, rejecting an established characteristic of the dominant culture when Jesus directly commissions the women "to go and tell" rather than instructing them to go get the men disciples first.

The Priest's Cover-up (Matthew 28:11-15)

While the women hurry away to fulfill their instructions, the guards are now faced with a dilemma. The closely guarded tomb is now empty. They inform the chief priests of the empty tomb and are offered money in exchange for claiming the disciples came and stole the body of Jesus. This text contains a Gnostic-Manipulationist discourse with the chief priests seeking to manipulate the situation in order to change the perceived outcome. Also, the chief priests enter into a dyadic contract when they offer money in exchange for the guards' false report. According to Robbins, a dyadic contract is an implicit contract entered into by two parties, unenforceable but bound by honor (Robbins, 1996). The chief priests represent the dominant culture, supported by the social structure and vested with power to impose their will on others. France pinpoints that the cover-up story is devised by the chief priests together with the elders, who have been mentioned frequently by Matthew as the natural allies of the priests in planning the elimination of Jesus; these two groups together represented the power structure focused on the temple to which Jesus had been so obvious a threat, so that it is in their interests to inflict damage upon the honor and credibility of the disciples (France, 2007).

The Messianic Mission (Matthew 28:16-20)

Matthew 28:16-20 would be identified as a conversionist response. As the followers of Jesus go into all the world and make disciples through conversion to Christianity, not only are the people changed but the world will change as well. These final words of Jesus as written by Matthew also identify a new purpose and the true mission of the kingdom message. In Matthew 15:24, Jesus states that He was sent to the lost sheep of the house of Israel (Spirit Filled Life Bible (NKJV), 1991). In Matthew 28:18-20, the vision is cast from the house of Israel to the entire world. According to Malina and Rohrbaugh, in this final edict of Matthew (28:16-20), the God who gives Jesus "all authority in heaven and on earth" is no longer simply YHWH or just the God of Israel, but the unique and single God of all humankind since discipleship is for "all nations," not just for a "chosen people." (Malina & Rohrbaugh, 1992). Additionally, Wright concludes that God purposed from the beginning to address and deal with the problems within His creation through Israel; Israel was not just to be an example of a nation under God but Israel was to be the means through which the world would be saved (Wright, 1999).

Credibility of the Kingdom Message

The credibility of this kingdom message continues beyond Matthew 28 and extends to this current age and time. Kouzes and Posner have identified the need that current leaders have for developing credibility by deriving their six disciplines of credibility, which are (Kouzes & Posner, 1993):

- Discovering Your Self
- Appreciating Your Constituents
- Affirming Shared Values

- Developing A Capacity
- Serving A Purpose
- Sustaining Hope

Leaders of organizations in today's environment can look at the life of Jesus as depicted in Matthew 28 and see an example of how Jesus demonstrated each of these disciplines thereby establishing His credibility according to Kouzes and Posner. To establish credibility, leaders must first clarify their values and standards (Kouzes & Posner, 1993). Jesus demonstrates this discipline by His resurrection and conquering death, dishonor, and the grave. By visibly appearing and talking to others, Jesus is demonstrating who He is and that He is the King of all kingdoms. Death could not hold Him down. He is the risen King.

Leadership is a relationship and strong relationships are built upon mutual trust and understanding; constituents come to believe in their leaders and to see them as worthy of their trust (Kouzes & Posner, 1993). Jesus demonstrates this discipline by appearing to both His female and male followers. He is showing the inclusion of all people and genders through His contact with each of them and taking the time to talk with all of them, which Galatians 3:28 records (Spirit Filled Life Bible (NKJV), 1991):

> There is neither Jew nor Greek, there is neither slave nor free, there is neither male nor female; for you are all one in Christ Jesus.

Affirming Shared Values

Credible leaders build a strong sense of community and find common ground to build a consensus around a core of shared values (Kouzes & Posner, 1993). In Matthew 28:18, Jesus came and spoke to them, saying, "All authority has been given to Me in heaven and on earth (Spirit Filled Life Bible (NKJV), 1991)." Jesus demonstrates this discipline by proclaiming the level and extent of His authority and then gives it to His disciples to use. He has won the victory and now shares this authority with the disciples enabling them to go about proclaiming the kingdom message.

To strengthen credibility, leaders must clearly articulate the aims and aspirations of the organization and the role of each constituent (Kouzes & Posner, 1993). In Matthew 28:19-20, Jesus clearly delineates the role of His disciples (Spirit Filled Life Bible (NKJV), 1991):

> Go therefore and make disciples of all the nations, baptizing them in the name of the Father and of the Son and of the Holy Spirit, teaching them to observe all things that I have commanded you.

Credible leaders lead by example and spend time expressing the value that each person brings to the organization; this team spirit works together for the good of all (Kouzes & Posner, 1993). Jesus expands the mission to carry His kingdom message out from the people of Israel to all people in the world because they are all His creation. He equips His disciples with His authority in order for them to go about doing the work of the kingdom on His behalf.

Sustaining Innovation

Credible leaders keep hope alive and provide energy, enthusiasm, inspiration, and optimism to their constituents (Kouzes & Posner, 1993). Jesus' last words to His disciples are filled with this discipline when He says, "Lo, I am with you always, even to the end of the age (Spirit Filled Life Bible (NKJV), 1991)." Matthew concludes his gospel with amen, so be it. Jesus was the right person at the right time to accomplish the mission of introducing the kingdom message. He was never "out-of-sync" with His heavenly Father. The mystery of the ages has been announced. The King has returned and through Israel the Kingdom of God has been expanded to all humankind. The gospel message is as credible today as it was then. Strategic leaders can learn from the example of Jesus as He demonstrated the six disciplines of credibility to His disciples. Credibility will strengthen the relationship between leaders and followers, and leaders of today can still learn these lessons from almost 2000 years ago. Additionally, through exegetical analysis it is revealed that Jesus' strategy is to change the people of all nations through the kingdom message not just the people of Israel. This is corroborated in the progression of discourse and rhetoric from thaumaturgical to counterculture, to gnostic-manipulationist to conversionist rhetoric. The Gospel of Matthew reveals Jesus as the King in His kingdom, His counter-cultural approach to the Romans as well as the religious leaders of the day and reveals His purpose to change the world with His kingdom message. Because of this counter-cultural revolution which changes the course of all mankind, Jesus is the greatest innovator of all time.

Chapter 18
Jesus is the Master Innovator

"A disciple is not above his teacher, or a slave above his master. It is enough for a disciple to become like his teacher and a slave like his master."
Matthew 10:24-25 (HCSB)

In the beginning was the Word, and the Word was with God, and the Word was God. He was with God in the beginning. All things were created through Him, and apart from Him not one thing was created that has been created. Life was in Him, and hat life was the light of men. That light shines in the darkness, yet the darkness did not overcome it.
John 1:1-5 (HCSB)

Jesus was present in the beginning of leadership through the present day. Not only is He the greatest innovator of all time producing a cultural change that has spread worldwide, but he is also the Master Innovator. All of the common core competencies in this book can be found in the life and times of Jesus of Nazareth. As a reminder, the 12 common cores of competencies identified in this book for innovative leaders to develop are:

1. Core Values
2. Creativity
3. Strategic Mindset
4. Redesign
5. Trust
6. Ethics

7. Context
8. Forecasting
9. Rest & Renewal
10. Leadership Succession
11. Mentoring/Discipling
12. Understanding People

Again, this list is not comprehensive but, at least, identifies a starting point to begin the process for emerging leaders to develop in the quest to become an innovative leader.

Jesus and the Common Core of Core Values

While core values seem to be more of a modern era concept, the reality of core values can be traced back to the beginning of time. With core values needing to be founded in an unchangeable source, Jesus and the Bible become the only logical sources. Jesus knew what was at His core, but it takes a Master Innovator to take the core values of an entire group of people that has gone astray, and return them to their original intent. This is what Jesus did in Matthew 22:34-40 when a group of Pharisees tried to ensnare Him (HCSB, 2010):

> When the Pharisees heard that He had silenced the Sadducees, they came together. And one of them, an expert in the law, asked a question to test Him: "Teacher, which command in the law is the greatest?" He said to him, "Love the Lord your God with all your heart, with all your soul, and with all your mind. This is the greatest and most important command. The second is like it: Love your neighbor as yourself. All the Law and the Prophets depend on these two commands."

Only Jesus could take on the entirety of Jewish Law, which is the very core of that culture that has gone away from its original purpose and bring into a single phrase the summation of the entire Old Covenant Law. Verse 40 is profound in stating, "All the Law and the Prophets depend on these two commands." It has been said that the first statement from Jesus covers the first five of the original Ten Commandments and the second statement the next five. However, Jesus boldly proclaims that these two statements cover not just all of the 10 Commandments, but all of the entire Law as well as everything the Prophets prophesied. The Apostle John later emphasizes this same truth and firmly establishes the core value of the Christian organization in 1 John 4:8, "The one who does not love does not know God, because God is love." Therefore, the core value of Jesus and all the Christian church is love.

Jesus and the Common Core of Creativity

As previously stated creativity originated with God when He spoke the world into existence and breathed life into man in the Book of Genesis. However, the common core of creativity mentioned here is much deeper. Only one thing can "top" the creation of man, and that is the re-creation of man. One of the top leaders of the Jewish people, Nicodemus, would visit Jesus at night as stated in John chapter three. Yet, the concept of salvation and being "born again" was beyond the grasp of one of the top Jewish teachers of the day. John 3:1-9 (HCSB, 2010):

> There was a man from the Pharisees named Nicodemus, a ruler of the Jews. This man came to Him at night and said, "Rabbi, we know that You have come from God as a teacher, for no one could perform these signs You do unless God were with him." Jesus replied, "I assure you: Unless someone is born again, he cannot see the kingdom of God." "But how can anyone be born when he is old?" Nicodemus asked Him. "Can he enter his mother's womb a second time and be born?" Jesus answered, "I assure you: Unless someone is born of water and the Spirit, he cannot enter the kingdom of God. Whatever is born of the flesh is flesh, and whatever is born of the Spirit is spirit. Do not be amazed that I told you that you must be born again. The wind blows where it pleases, and you hear its sound, but you don't know where it comes from or where it is going. So it is with everyone born of the Spirit." "How can these things be?" asked Nicodemus.

Nicodemus was unable to understand the re-creation of a person through the salvation experience of becoming born again; yet, children as young as three have accepted the free gift that Jesus offers through salvation. Children in Sunday School can explain this simple, but profound, concept that Nicodemus struggled to understand. Paul re-affirmed this concept to the Corinthians in 2 Corinthians 5:17, "Therefore, if anyone is in Christ, he is a new creation; old things have passed away, and look, new things have come." Only Jesus as the Master Innovator could introduce a re-creation experience.

Jesus and the Common Core of the Strategic Mindset

A strategic mindset is the product of strategic thinking and strategic planning. The seeds of the long range plan were first planted in the Garden of Eden from Genesis 3:13-15 (HCSB, 2010):

> So the Lord God asked the woman, "What is this you have done?" And the woman said, "It was the serpent. He deceived me, and I ate." Then the Lord God said to the serpent: Because you have done this, you are cursed more than any livestock and more than any wild animal. You will move on your belly and eat dust all the days of your life. I will put hostility between you and the woman, and between your seed and her seed. He will strike your head, and you will strike his heel.

The strategic plan to redeem mankind is announced in the first of many prophecies concerning the coming Messiah. Prophecies continue for the next thousands of years and culminate at the crucifixion and resurrection of the Messiah to redeem mankind back to the Father.

Jesus and the Common Core of Redesign

From an organizational point of view, Jesus was looking at an organization that needed a counter cultural approach to make a permanent change in the Kingdom of God. The "old" way of doing business was no longer adequate and complete redesign was in the CEO's (God the Father) long range plan. Jesus was to be the agent of change, and the Holy Spirit would be given to continue the work. The organization needed a catalyst to shift from the Old Covenant to the New Covenant to complete the redesign. For this organization, two catalysts were provided the crucifixion/resurrection of Jesus and the infilling of the Holy Spirit on the Day of Pentecost in Acts 2:1-4 (HCSB, 2010):

> When the day of Pentecost had arrived, they were all together in one place. Suddenly a sound like that of a violent rushing wind came from heaven, and it filled the whole house where they were staying. And tongues, like flames of fire that were divided, appeared to them and rested on each one of them. Then they were all filled with the Holy Spirit and began to speak in different languages, as the Spirit gave them ability for speech.

The next phase of the redesign is complete and the Church age is established. The final phase of redesign is yet to come and many events are still part of the strategic plan of God. Revelation 21:1-4 (HCSB, 2010):

> Then I saw a new heaven and a new earth, for the first heaven and the first earth had passed away, and the sea no longer existed. I also saw the Holy City, new Jerusalem, coming down out of heaven from God, prepared like a bride adorned for her husband. Then I heard a loud voice from the throne: Look! God's dwelling is with humanity, and He will live with them. They will be His people, and God Himself will be with them and be their God. He will wipe away every tear from their eyes. Death will no longer exist; grief, crying, and pain will exist no longer, because the previous things have passed away.

The strategic plan started in the Garden of Eden will eventually come full circle.

Jesus and the Common Core of Trust

Trust is a two-way relationship. Jesus shows His trust in His disciples to continue the work after His departure when He gives them the Great Commission in Matthew 28:16-20 (HCSB, 2010):

> The 11 disciples traveled to Galilee, to the mountain where Jesus had directed them. When they saw Him, they worshiped, but some doubted. Then Jesus came near and said to them, "All authority has been given to Me in heaven and on earth. Go, therefore, and make disciples of all nations, baptizing them in the name of the Father and of the Son and of the Holy Spirit, teaching them to observe everything I have commanded you. And remember, I am with you always, to the end of the age."

Many organizations falter and fail after the founding leader moves on. However, the Church as an organization has grown from one person, Jesus, to a worldwide organization in the millions. The disciples demonstrate their trust in Jesus by believing His words and going forth as He directed. Perhaps Corrie ten Boom best captured the essence of trust from mankind's point of view when she said, "Never be afraid to trust an unknown future to a known God."

Jesus and the Common Core of Ethics

Ethics are behaviors that affect the heart and are translated into morals to live by; they are not just a religious exercise in semantics. Christian ethics result from a personal relationship with Jesus Christ which supernaturally empowers you to change from sinner to saint and enables you to live a life above reproach. "Religion" encompasses a set of rules to live by without the relationship or the power to live them. Many of the Jewish leaders in the time of Jesus had the written Law to follow, but their hearts did not have His writings written upon them. John 12:39-41 best describes this condition (HCSB, 2010):

> This is why they were unable to believe, because Isaiah also said: He has blinded their eyes and hardened their hearts, so

> that they would not see with their eyes or understand with their hearts, and be converted, and I would heal them. Isaiah said these things because he saw His glory and spoke about Him.

Ethical living begins as a "head" condition, but in order to live by ethics it must also become a "heart" condition. Jesus understood that mankind needed their hearts changed as well as their mind renewed. Salvation was provided to change the heart condition, and Paul describes how to renew the mind in Romans 12:1-2 (HCSB, 2010):

> Therefore, brothers, by the mercies of God, I urge you to present your bodies as a living sacrifice, holy and pleasing to God; this is your spiritual worship. Do not be conformed to this age, but be transformed by the renewing of your mind, so that you may discern what is the good, pleasing, and perfect will of God.

As Christian believers read the Scriptures and align their service to the Lord according to His purpose, then the mind is renewed or re-programmed according to the plan and purpose of God the Father. Hearts and minds that are rooted in themselves through secular humanism will constantly battle the ethics question due to their standards being subjective and relative.

Jesus and the Common Core of Context

While the teachings of Jesus are timeless and universal, it is vital to understand the context of the time that He walked the earth. This is especially true in understanding the counter-cultural revolution that He sparked. Wright contends that Jesus introduced a counter-cultural movement during the Second Temple Period by going out among the people in the local villages and demonstrating the power of God through healings, miracles, signs, and wonders; he believed Jesus was emphasizing that the Kingdom was at hand, and all were invited to join (Wright, 1999). It is equally crucial to realize that the Israeli people were looking for someone to setup a physical kingdom like King David's and remove the

Roman rule of the day. It has been postulated by some that Judas Iscariot had become disillusioned by the lack of a physical kingdom as an answer to his betrayal. Regardless of this, Jesus had to teach and promote the kingdom of God in a context that was counter to the prevalent mindset of the day. Wright further adds that the Jewish people began looking for the return of a King that would bring peace to the land of Israel which had survived the Babylonian captivity and the rule of the Persians, Greeks, Syrians, and finally the Romans (Wright,1998).

An understanding of the context of Jewish culture would also help many modern day students of the Bible gain insight into the parables and teachings of Jesus. His goal was not to just speak as the Scribes, Pharisees, and Sadducees, but to teach with authority to the common people as described in Matthew 7:28-29 (HCSB, 2010):

> When Jesus had finished this sermon, the crowds were astonished at His teaching, because He was teaching them like one who had authority, and not like their scribes.

Of course, nothing is worse than taking Scripture out of context simply to convey a pre-determined meaning. The classic example of Scripture being taken out of context mixes the passages that relate to Judas Iscariot going out to hang himself, and adding the passage that this is the will of God for your life: "Judas hanged himself...go and do ye likewise." Not a good combination.

Jesus and the Common Core of Forecasting

Forecasting and foresight are closely related futures and future determinations. From early in His ministry, Jesus spoke of future events like the one in John 2:18-21 (HCSB, 2010):

> So the Jews replied to Him, "What sign of authority will You show us for doing these things?" Jesus answered, "Destroy this sanctuary, and I will raise it up in three days." Therefore the Jews said, "This sanctuary took 46 years to build, and will You raise it up in three days?" But He was speaking about the

> sanctuary of His body. So when He was raised from the dead, His disciples remembered that He had said this. And they believed the Scripture and the statement Jesus had made.

One of the keys for the use of forecasting is to look into a possible future to make decisions in the present. Jesus wanted to ensure that His disciples understood that when He went away, they would not be alone. This is recorded in John 14:15-18 (HCSB, 2010):

> "If you love Me, you will keep My commands. And I will ask the Father, and He will give you another Counselor to be with you forever. He is the Spirit of truth. The world is unable to receive Him because it doesn't see Him or know Him. But you do know Him, because He remains with you and will be in you. I will not leave you as orphans; I am coming to you."

Jesus and the Common Core of Rest and Renewal

Jesus spent much of His time teaching His disciples and ministering to the people. However, He also took time apart to rest and refresh Himself with the Father. One instance is when John the Baptist was beheaded as recorded in Matthew 14:10-13 (HCSB, 2010):

> So he [Herod] sent orders and had John beheaded in the prison. His head was brought on a platter and given to the girl, who carried it to her mother. Then his disciples came, removed the corpse, buried it, and went and reported to Jesus. When Jesus heard about it, He withdrew from there by boat to a remote place to be alone.

Rather than to respond or react to this event, Jesus choose to withdraw and recompose. Jesus does respond later in this chapter by feeding the 5000. After this time of ministry, He returned to a time of rest and prayer in John 14:22-23 (HCSB, 2010):

> Immediately He made the disciples get into the boat and go ahead of Him to the other side, while He dismissed the

> crowds. After dismissing the crowds, He went up on the mountain by Himself to pray. When evening came, He was there alone.

Hebrews 4:1 later records that some rest is only found in the Lord when it states, "Therefore, while the promise to enter His rest remains; let us fear that none of you should miss it."

Jesus and the Common Core of Leadership Succession

For leadership to continue, successors have to be identified and trained. Jesus chose the original 12 disciples to teach and leave the work of the ministry. As with many succession plans, some do not follow through to the end. Judas Iscariot forfeits his seat, which is later filled by Matthias in Acts 1:23-26 (HCSB, 2010):

> So they proposed two: Joseph, called Barsabbas, who was also known as Justus, and Matthias. Then they prayed, "You, Lord, know the hearts of all; show which of these two You have chosen to take the place in this apostolic service that Judas left to go to his own place." Then they cast lots for them, and the lot fell to Matthias. So he was numbered with the 11 apostles.

Jesus also called others to come along side of Him, but they held back. The rich young ruler is an example of this in Mark 10:

> He said to Him, "Teacher, I have kept all these from my youth." Then, looking at him, Jesus loved him and said to him, "You lack one thing: Go, sell all you have and give to the poor, and you will have treasure in heaven. Then come, follow Me." But he was stunned at this demand, and he went away grieving, because he had many possessions.

The same command of "come follow Me" are the words that Jesus used to call His other disciples. However, this young man could not—at least at that time. The original disciples were crucial in their participation to announce that the Kingdom of heaven was at hand and that salvation was available to the Jews who believed. However, the final man recorded in the Gospels for Jesus to call personally and directly was Saul of Tarsus. His dramatic conversion on the road to Damascus was required for his daunting assignment to bring the entire world in to the saving knowledge of Jesus Christ. Saul became the Apostle Paul's, and his assignment is recorded in Acts 9:15-16: "But the Lord said to him, "Go, for he is a chosen vessel of Mine to bear My name before Gentiles, kings, and the children of Israel. For I will show him how many things he must suffer for My name's sake."

Jesus and the Common Core of Mentoring and Discipling

Proper mentoring requires spending time with the "mentorees". Jesus spent approximately 3.5 years teaching, demonstrating and manifesting the power of God and the Kingdom of God to the original 12 disciples. Mark 4:10-11 describes this (HCSB, 2010):

> When He was alone with the Twelve, those who were around Him asked Him about the parables. He answered them, "The secret of the kingdom of God has been given to you, but to those outside, everything comes in parables.

From the outset of Jesus' ministry, He was establishing disciples through His teaching. John 8:31-32 (HCSB, 2010):

> As He was saying these things, many believed in Him. So Jesus said to the Jews who had believed Him, "If you continue in My word, you really are My disciples. You will know the truth, and the truth will set you free."

Knowledge of the truth produces freedom, and believing in the truths that Jesus taught produces disciples. This process continues today. As we read the words of Jesus, believe, and act upon them, we become His disciples to a new generation.

Jesus and the Common Core of Understanding People

More than anyone else that has ever walked on this earth, Jesus understood people. The author of the book of Hebrews, presumed to be the Apostle Paul, describes Jesus in His role as High Priest, "This High Priest of ours understands our weaknesses, for he faced all of the same testings we do, yet he did not sin" (Hebrews 4:15, NLT). He could not only read their outward behavior, but He knew their heart, thoughts, and motives as described in Matthew 9:4-8 (HCSB, 2010):

> But perceiving their thoughts, Jesus said, "Why are you thinking evil things in your hearts?" For which is easier: to say, 'Your sins are forgiven,' or to say, 'Get up and walk'? But so you may know that the Son of Man has authority on earth to forgive sins"—then He told the paralytic, "Get up, pick up your mat, and go home." And he got up and went home. When the crowds saw this, they were awestruck and gave glory to God who had given such authority to men.

Due to the fact that Jesus is Word of God made flesh as stated in John 1:14, He has the ability to understand the most inward motivations of people. As it states in Hebrews 4:12, "For the word of God is living and powerful, and sharper than any two-edged sword, piercing even to the division of soul and spirit, and of joints and marrow, and is a discerner of the thoughts and intents of the heart."

Because of His understanding of people, He always knew how to manage delicate situations such as the one in John 8:6-11 (HCSB, 2010):

> Jesus stooped down and started writing on the ground with His finger. When they persisted in questioning Him, He stood up and said to them, "The one without sin among you should be the first to throw a stone at her." Then He stooped down again and continued writing on the ground. When they heard this, they left one by one, starting with the older men. Only He was left, with the woman in the center. When Jesus stood up, He said to her, "Woman, where are they? Has no one

condemned you?" "No one, Lord," she answered. "Neither do I condemn you," said Jesus. "Go, and from now on do not sin anymore."

Following Jesus

From the handling of the crowd wanting to stone the young woman to her ultimate conversion, Jesus understood people. Throughout the Gospels, there is a clarion call to follow Christ which is followed by a call in the epistles to follow delegated Christian leadership as they follow the Lord. In other words, the Christian admonition came from the apostle Paul in 1 Corinthians 11:1, "Be ye followers of me, even as I also am of Christ" (KJV). Christians are to be Christ-like and become leaders who are Christ-like. From the DISC model perspective, Jesus actually operated in all four personality types; His leadership style could be direct and demanding, inspiring and influential, steady and stable, cautious and compliant depending upon the situation.

Like Jesus, leaders should strive to develop these 12 common core competences in their lives. After all, leadership existed in the beginning and continues today. Adding these common cores will help leaders move towards becoming emerging innovative leaders in their lives and careers.

The Charge to Become an Innovative Leader

Ralph Waldo Emerson once penned, "We change, whether we like it or not." Change is a fact of existence on this earth; hence, world-changers or innovators are in high demand to facilitate transitions in politics, business, religion, and all other areas of life. Through this study, twelve common cores have been delineated to equip the leaders of today to become the innovators of tomorrow.

Much has been written about innovation; however, never before have traits been synthesized into select common cores competencies for emerging innovative leaders. These core characteristics have been extracted from a wealth of material from the world's greatest thinkers and have been condensed into a workable development plan to assure future success.

Developing these competencies in today's leaders will assure transitional success in entities from the smallest to the largest—from families to nations. In the Old Testament, Moses' father-in-law, Jethro, determined a plan to develop leaders to supervise tens, fifties, hundreds, etc. Whether a group is small or large, a leader is needed to guide and direct that group in order to harness the energy of the individuals to become a force of power to elicit needed change to ensure longevity and to accomplish their stated purpose.

Whether a captain of ten or a captain of thousands, relying only on natural leadership abilities is unwise and limiting. A strategic plan determined to develop informed and equipped leaders is necessary in our changing world. As Mahatma Gandhi said, "We must become the change we want to see." Academies must educate, organizations must invest, and individuals must heed the charge to develop the stated competencies needed for the world's upcoming leaders:

1. Core Values
2. Creativity
3. Strategic Mindset
4. Redesign
5. Trust
6. Ethics
7. Context
8. Forecasting
9. Rest & Renewal
10. Leadership Succession
11. Mentoring/Discipling
12. Understanding People

This common core of competencies for emerging innovative leaders has been developed to establish and fortify the force of change in our human culture. Success of an individual has not always assured the success of an organization; however, with these core characteristics, individual leadership success will be assured in conjunction with organizational success. With a level of proficiency in these aptitudes, change can be embraced, and evolution for impact on the future will be guaranteed.

About the Author

DARRELL PARSONS is a military officer, educator, Bible teacher, and businessman. He lives with his wife and daughter in Virginia. Darrell has been a Christian for over forty years and continues to be involved in ministry as he has for the last twenty-five years.

Dr. Parsons has been involved in team building through understanding personalities in varied capacities. Throughout his career, he has worked in educational, military, church, and business environments.

As a veteran author, this third book follows the publishing of *Release Your Words—Impact Your World* and *Why Do I Do the Things I Do?*. Darrell earned a Masters in Education from the University of Tennessee and a Doctorate of Strategic Leadership (DSL) from Regent University.

From his varied background and training, Darrell offers a unique insight into developing leaders and helping people reclaim their voices.

References

Aaltio-Marjosola, I., & Takala, T. (2000). Charismatic Leadership, Manipulation and the Complexity of Organizational Life. *Journal of Workplace Learning*, 12(4), 146-158 DOI: 10.1108/13665620010332750.

Air Force Times. (2004). Retrieved August 1, 2011, from http://www.airforcetimes.com/legacy/new/0-AIRPAPER-487000.php

Amazon. (2013). Retrieved October 11, 2013, from http://www.amazon.com/s/ref=nb_sb_noss?url=search-alias%3Ddigital-text&field-keywords=

American Booksellers Association. (1996). *The 1996 Consumer Research Study on Book Publishing*. New York: American Booksellers Association.

Appelbaum, S. H., St-Pierre, N., & Glavas, W. (1998). Strategic Organizational Change: The Role of Leadership, Learning, Motivation and Productivity. *Management Decision*, 36(5), 289 -301 DOI: 10.1108/00251749810220496.

Archaeological Study Bible NIV. (2005). Grand Rapids: Zondervan.

Ashkenas, R., Ulrich, D., Jick, T., & Kerr, S. (2002). *The Boundaryless Organization: Breaking the Chains of Organizational Structure*. San Francisco: Jossey-Bass.

Avrin, L. (1991). Scribes, Script and Books: The Book Arts from Antiquity to the Renaissance. New York: American Library Association.

Baez-Camargo, G. (1986). *Archaeological Commentary on the Bible*. New York: Doubleday-Galilee Books.

Barnes & Noble. (2011). Retrieved October 11, 2013, from http://bookclubs.barnesandnoble.com/t5/NOOK-Color-General-Discussion/B-amp-N-Says-There-Are-Over-2-Million-Books-Available/td-p/790676

Bass, B. (1990). From Transactional to Transformational Leadership: Learning to Share the Vision. *Organizational Dynamics*, 18(3), 19-31.

Bass, B. (2008). *The Bass Handbook of Leadership*. New York: Free Press.

Bell, C. R. (2002). *Managers as Mentors*. San Francisco: Berrett-Koehler Publishers Inc.

Bell, M., & Tunnicliff, G. (1996). Future Search for Stakeholders. *Management Development Review*, 9(1), 13-16.

Bennis, W. (1999). The End of Leadership: Exemplary Leadership Is Impossible without Full Inclusion, Initiatives, and Cooperation of Followers. *Organizational Dynamics*, 28(1), 71-79 DOI: 10.1016/S0090-2616(00)80008-X.

Bennis, W. (2000). Breaking the Code of Change. (M. Beer, & N. Nohria, Eds.) Cambridge: Harvard Business School.

Bennis, W. G. (1992). *On Becoming a Leader.* Wilmington: Addison-Wesley.

Bingham, T., & Galagan, P. (2010). Be More Innovative: An Interview with Dan Cathy. T+D, 64(3), 36-41.

Black, J. S., Morrison, A. J., & Gregersen, H. B. (1999). *Global Explorers: The Next Generation of Leaders.* New York: Routledge.

Blackaby, H. T., & Blackaby, R. (2001). *Spiritual Leadership.* Nashville: Broadman and Holman Publishers.

Block, P. (2001). *The Flawless Consutling Fieldbook and Companion*. San Francisco: Jossey-Bass/Pfeiffer.

Bloom, B. S. (1971). *Mastery Learning: Theory and Practice.* New York City: Holt Rinehart & Winston.

Blume, K. A. (2012, July 16). *Baptist Press.* Retrieved August 4, 2012, from http://www.bpnews.net/bpnews.asp?id=38271

Bolme, S. (2006). *Your Guide to Marketing Books in the Christian Marketplace.* Charlotte: Crest Publications.

Bosman, J. (2012). *NY Times.* Retrieved October 11, 2013, from http://www.nytimes.com/2012/01/29/business/barnes-noble-taking-on-amazon-in-the-fight-of-its life.html?_r=4&pagewanted=all?src=tp

Bossidy, L., & Charan, R. (2002). Execution: *The Discipline of Getting Things Done.* New York: Crown Publishing Group.

Bowkers. (2011). *Bowker's Annual Book Production Report.* New Providence: Bowkers.

Branson, C. M. (2009). *Leadership for an Age of Wisdom.* New York: Springer Science+Business Media.

Briner, B., & Pritchard, R. (1998). *Leadership Lessons of Jesus.* New York, NY: Gramercy Books .

Brown, M. (1989). Ethics in Organizations . *Issues in Ethic*, 2(1), 3-6.

Buckler, B. (1996). A Learning Process Model to Achieve Continuous Improvement and Innovation. The Learning Organization, 3(3), 31–39.

Burns, J. M. (1978). *Leadership.* New York: Harper& Row.

BusinessDictionary.com. (2012). Retrieved June 13, 2012, from http://www.businessdictionary.com/definition/gatekeeper.html

Cameron, K. S., & Quinn, R. E. (2011). *Diagnosing and Changing Organizational Culture Based on the Competing Values Framework* (3rd ed.). San Francisco: Jossey-Bass.

Canton, J. (2006). *The Extreme Future: The Top Trends that will Reshape the World for the next 5, 10, and 20 Years.* New York: Dutton.

Carbonell, M. (1993). *Solving the Mystery of Motivation*. Fayetteville, GA: Institute of Leadership Technology.

Castledale Inc. (2008). *A Strategic Study for the Book Publishing Industry in Ontario.* Ontario, Canada: Castledale Inc.

Catholic Encyclopedia. (2009). Retrieved June 11, 2012, from http://www.newadvent.org/cathen/14727b.htm

Cathy, T. (1989). *It's Easier to Succeed that to Fail.* Nashville: Oliver-Nelson Books.

Cheng, C. (1998). Uniform Change: An Ethnography on Organizational Symbolism, Volunteer Motivation and Dysfunctional Change in a Paramilitary Organization. *Leadership & Organization Development Journal*, 19(1), 22-31 DOI: 10.1108/01437739810368802.

Chermack, T. J. (2011). *Scenario Planning in Organizations*. San Francisco: Berrett-Koehler Publishers, Inc.

Ciulla, J. (Ed.). (2004). *Ethics, the Heart of Leadership*. Westport: Praeger Publishers.

Cockerell, L. (2008). *Creating Magic: 10 Common Sense Leadership Strategies from a Life at Disney.* New York: Doubleday.

Cohen, S. L. (2010). Effective Global Leadership Requires a Global Mindset. *Industrial and Commercial Training*, 42(1), 3-10.

Cohen, W. A. (1998). *The Stuff of Heroes: The Eight Universal Laws of Leadership.* Marietta, GA: Longstreet.

Cooper, J. R. (1998). A Multidimensional Approach to the Adoption of Innovation. Management Decision, 36(8), 493-502 DOI: 10.1108/00251749810232565.

Cornish, E. (2005). *Futuring: The Exploration of the Future*. Bethesda: World Future Society.

Covey, S. (1989). *The 7 Habits of Highly Effective People.* New York, NY: Fireside.

Cummings, O. (2004). *Deacons of the Church.* New York: Paulist Press.

Daft, R. L. (2007). *Organization Theory and Design* (9th ed.). Mason, OH: Thomson South-Western.

Darling, J. R., & Heller, V. L. (2011). Managing Conflict with the Chinese: The Key from an In-Depth Single Case Study. *Chinese Management Studies*, 5(1), 35-54 DO: 10.1108/17506141111118444.

de Kluyver, C. A., & Pearce II, J. A. (2012). *Strategy: A View from the Top*. Upper Saddle River, NJ: Pearson Education Inc.

Deming, W. E. (1994). *The New Economics For Industry, Government, Education* (2 ed.). Cambridge: Massachusetts Institute of Technology.

DeSilva, D. A. (2004). *An Introduction to the New Testament Contexts, Methods & Ministry Formation*. Downers Grove: InterVarsity Press.

Disney Institute. (2001). *Be Our Guest*. New York: Disney Editions.

Dolan, S. L., & Richley, B. A. (2006). Management by Values (MBV): A New Philosophy for a New Economic Order. *Handbook of Business Strategy*, 7(1), 235-238 DOI: 10.1108/10775730610618873.

Eisner, M. (1999). *A Work in Progress*. London: Penguin Books.

Elmer, D. (1993). *Cross-Cultural Conflict: Building Relationships for Effective Ministry*. Downers Grove: InterVarsity Press.

Elmuti, D., & Kathawala, Y. (2001). An Overview of Strategic Alliances. *Management Decision*, 39(3), 205-218 DOI: 10.1108/EUM0000000005452.

Elwell, W. A., & Yarbrough, R. W. (1998). *Encountering the New Testament A Historical and Theological Survey*. Grand Rapids: Baker Books.

Emerald Group Publishing. (2011). Joint Effort: Integrating Leadership Development and Organizational Change. *Strategic Direction*, 27(1), 18-20 DOI: 10.1108/02580541111096566.

Encyclopedia Britannica. (2013). Retrieved October 1, 2013, from http://www.britannica.com/EBchecked/topic/482597/history-of-publishing/28597/Book-publishing

Finzel, H. (1994). *The Top Ten Mistakes Leaders Make*. Wheaton, IL: Victor Books.

Fletcher, B., & Jones, F. (1992). Measuring Organizational Culture: The Cultural Audit. *Managerial Auditing Journal*, 7(6), 30-37.

Foreman, K. (1999). Evolving Global Structures and the Challenges Facing International Relief and Development Organizations. *Nonprofit and Voluntary Sector Quarterly*, 28(4), 178–197.

France, R. T. (2007). The Gospel of Matthew (*The New International Commentary on the New Testament*) (Kindle ed.). Grand Rapids: William B. Eerdmans Publishing Company.

Freeman, J. M. (1972). *Manners and Customs of the Bible*. Plainfield, NJ: Logos International.

Frynas, J. G. (1998). Political Instability and Business: Focus on Shell in Nigeria. *Third World Quarterly*, 19(3), 457-478 DOI:10.1080/01436599814343.

Fua, S. J. (2007). Looking Towards the Source – Social Justice and Leadership Conceptualisations from Tonga. *Journal of Educational Administration*, 45(6), 672-683 DOI: 10.1108/09578230710829865.

Fuller, B. (1975). *Synergetics—Explorations in the Geometry of Thinking*. New York: Macmillan Publishing.

Gabler, N. (2007). *Walt Disney*. New York: Vintage Books.

Gabrielsson, J., & Politis, D. (2009). Entrepreneurs' Attitudes Towards Failure: An Experiential Learning Approach. *International Journal of Entrepreneurial Behaviour & Research*, 15(4), 364 - 383 DOI: 10.1108/13552550910967921.

Galbraith, J. (2002). *Designing Organizations: An Executive Guide to Strategy*, Structure, and Process. San Francisco: Jossey-Bass.

Galbraith, J. R. (2000). *Designing the Global Corporation*. San Francisco: John Wiley & Sons, Inc.

Gangel, K. O. (1981). *Building Leaders for Church Education*. Chicago: Moody Press.

Garavan, T. N., & Deegan, J. (1995). Discontinuous Change in Organizations: Using Training and Development Interventions to Develop Creativity. *Industrial and Commercial Training*, 27(11), 18-25 DOI: 10.1108/00197859510147607.

Gary, J. (2008). The Future According to Jesus: A Galilean Model of Foresight. *Futures*, 40(7), 630-642 DOI:10.1016/j.futures.2007.12.004.

George, B. (2007). *True North: Discover Your Authentic Leadership*. San Francisco: Jossey-Bass.

Ghislanzoni, G., Heidari-Robinson, S., & Jermiin, M. (December 2010). Taking Organizational Redesigns from Plan to Practice. *McKinsey Quarterly*, 1-9.

Gower, R. (1987). *The New Manners and Customs of Bible Times*. Chicago: Moody Press.

Graham, R. (1981). The Role of Perception of Time in Consumer Research. *Journal of Consumer Research*(7), 335-342.

Greco, A. (2011). *Book Business.* Retrieved October 5, 2013, from http://www.bookbusinessmag.com/article/ebooks-by-numbers/1

Greenberger, D., & Thoms, P. (1995). The Relationship Between Leadership and Time Orientation. *Journal of Management Inquiry,* 4(3), 272-292.

Gregson, K. (1994). Mentoring. *Journal of Workplace Learning,* 6(4), 26-27 DOI: 10.1108/13665629410071225.

Grocock, A. (2002). Universities in the Future. *Journal of the Royal Society of Medicine,* 95(1), 48-49.

Gryskiewicz, S. (1999). *Positive Turbulence: Developing Climates for Creativity, Innovation, and Renewal.* San Francisco: Jossey Bass.

Gudykunst, W. B., & Kim, Y. Y. (2003). *Communicating with Strangers.* New York: McGraw-Hill.

Gunn, B. G. (2004). *Instructions of Ptah Hotep.* Retrieved July 1, 2014, from http://www.kenseamedia.com/encyclopedia/ppp/instructions_ptah_hotep.htm.

Gupta, A. (2008). International Trends and Private Higher Education in India. *International Journal of Educational Management,* 22(6), 565-594 DOI: 10.1108/09513540810895462.

Gyertson, D. J. (Ed.). (1993). *Salt & Light: A Christian Response to Current Issues.* Dallas: Word Publishing.

Hall, E. (1976). *Beyond Culture.* New York: Anchor Books.

Hall, E. (1989). *Beyond Culture.* New York: Anchor Press.

Halley, H. H. (1980). *Halley's Bible Handbook.* Grand Rapids, MI: Zondervan Publishing House.

Hamel, G. (2000). *Leading the Revolution.* Boston: Harvard Business School Press.

Harrison, E. F. (1995). Strategic Planning Maturities. *Management Decision,* 33(2), 48-55.

Hauschildt, J., & Schewe, G. (2000). Gatekeeper and Process Promotor: Key Persons in Agile and Innovative Organizations. *International Journal of Agile Management Systems,* 2(2), 96-103 DOI: 10.1108/14654650010312624.

Hayford, J. (1995). *Hayford's Bible Handbook.* Nashville: Thomas Nelson.

HCSB. (2010). *Holman Christian Standard Bible* (Kindle Edition). Nashville: B & H Publishing Group.

Hendricks, H. G., & Hendricks, W. D. (1995). *As Iron Sharpens Iron*. Chicago: Moody Press.

Heracleos, L. (1998). Strategic Thinking or Strategic Planning. *Long Range Planning*, 31(3), 481-487.

Hersey, P., & Blanchard, K. (1969). Life cycle theory of leadership. *Training & Development Journal*, Vol 23(5), 26-34.

Hines, A. (2006). Strategic Foresight. *The Futurist*(September- October), 18-21.

Hines, A., & Bishop, P. (Eds.). (2006). *Thinking About the Future: Guidelines for Strategic Foresight*. Washington: Social Technologies, LLC.

Ho, V. L., & Sculli, D. (1998). The Strategic Insights of Sun Tzu and Quality Management. *The TQM Magazine*, 10(3), 161 - 168 DOI: 10.1108/09544789810214774.

Hofstede, G. (1984). *Culture's Consequences: International Differences in Work Related Values*. Newbury Park: SAGE Publications Inc.

Hofstede, G. (1993). Cultural Constraints in Management Theories. *The Executive*, 7(1), 81-94.

Hofstede, G. (2001). *Culture's Consequences* (2nd ed.). Thousand Oaks: Sage.

Horsley, R. A., & Silberman, N. A. (2002). *The Message and the Kingdom*. Minneapolis: Fortress Press.

Houghton, J. D., & DiLiello, T. C. (2010). Leadership Development: The Key to Unlocking Individual Creativity in Organizations. *Leadership & Organization Development Journal*, 31(3), 230 - 245 DOI: 10.1108/01437731011039343.

Hughes, R. L., & Beatty, K. C. (2005). *Becoming A Strategic Leader: Your Role in Your Organization's Enduring Success*. San Francisco: Jossey-Bass.

Hunter, S., Steinberg, P., & Taylor, M. (2012). *Shifting to a Strategy of Innovation: The Key Role of Leadership in Consumer Packaged Goods*. State College: Penn State Executive Program.

Irvine, G. (1996). *Best Things in the Worst Times: An Insiders View of World Vision*. Wilsonville, Oregon: BookPartners, Inc.

Isherwood, A. (2011). *Strategy Tool Usage: What Tools Do Practicing Managers Use?* Retrieved February 16, 2012, from http://www.aiconsortia.com/documents/strategy-tool-usage-survey.pdf

Jarzabkowski, P., Giulietti, M., & Oliveira, B. (2011). *Advanced Institute of Management Research.* Retrieved October 16, 2013, from http://www.aimresearch.org/uploads/File/Publications/Executive%20 Briefings%202/Building_a_strategy_toolkit.pdf

Joas, H. (2000). *The Genesis of Values.* Chicago: University of Chicago Press.

Johanson, U., Skoog, M., Backlund, A., & Almqvist, R. (2006). Balancing Dilemmas of the Balanced Scorecard. *Accounting, Auditing & Accountability Journal,* 19(6), 842-857 DOI: 10.1108/09513570610709890.

Jones, R. (2010). *Army MWR.* Retrieved August 1, 2011, from http://www.armymwr.com/UserFiles/file/Commander/Travel_Guide-5_4c.pdf

Joseph, E. E., & Winston, B. E. (2005). A Correlation of Servant Leadership, Leader Trust, and Organizational Trust. *Leadership & Organization Development Journal,* 26(1), 6 - 22 DOI: 10.1108/01437730510575552.

Kaniss, A. (2006). Achieving a good P/PC balance. *Comprint Military Publications*, 3-4.

Kaplan, R., & Norton, D. (2001). The Strategy-Focused Organization. *Strategy & Leadership*, 29(3), 41-2.

Keidel, R. W. (1995). *Seeing Organizational Patterns.* San Francisco: Berrett-Koehler Publishers.

Khurana, R. (2002). *Searching for a Corporate Savior: The Irrational Quest for Charismatic CEOs.* Princeton: Princeton Press.

Kotter, J. P. (2005). Change Leadership. Leadership Excellence, 22(12), 3-4.

Kouzes, J. M., & Posner, B. Z. (1993). *Credibility: How Leaders Gain and Lose It, Why People Demand It.* San Francisco: Jossey-Bass Inc.

Kuczmarski, S. S., & Kuczmarski, T. D. (1995). *Values-Based Leadership.* Englewood Cliffs: Prentice Hall.

LaChance, S. (2006). Applying the Balanced Scorecard. *Strategic HR Review,* 5(2), 7.

LaHaye, T. (1983). *Transformed Temperaments.* Wheaton, IL: Tyndale House Publishers.

Lam, Y. (2002). Defining the Effects of Transformational Leadership on Organisational Learning: A Cross-Cultural Comparison. : *School Leadership and Management,* 22(4), 439-452 DOI: 10.1080/1363243022000053448.

Leadership Talks. (2007). Retrieved July 7, 2014, from http://www.regent.edu/admin/media/mp3/schgle/mentoring_discipling.mp3.

Lee, K. (1997). The Church Leaders and the Congregation. *CPC2 Worship Bulletin, Charis Methodist Church, Singapore*, 7-10.

Lehn, K., & Makhija, A. K. (1996). EVA & MVA as Performance Measures and Signals for Strategic Change. *Strategy & Leadership*, 24(3), 15-16.

Lewis, C. (1972). *Mere Christianity*. New York: Macmillan.

Lewis, C. (2002). *God in the Dock*. Grand Rapids: Eerdmans.

Littauer, F., & Littauer, M. (2006). *Communication Plus.* Ventura, CA: Regal Books.

Liu, C., Yu, Z., & Tjosvold, D. (2002). Production and People Values: Their Impact on Relationships and Leader Effectiveness in China. *Leadership & Organization Development Journal*, 23(3), 134-144 DOI: 10.1108/01437730210424075.

Locke, E. A., & Jain, V. K. (1995). Organizational Learning and Continuous Improvement. *International Journal of Organizational Analysis*, 3(1), 45-68 DOI:10.1108/eb028823.

Loo, T. (2006). *How to Define Your Life Purpose.* Retrieved September 3, 2013, from http://ezinearticles.com/?How-to-Define-Your-Life-Purpose&id=331527

Low, S. P. (1999). Towards Managerial Efficacy: Back to 2,000-Year-Old Guiding Principles. *Learning Organization*, 6(3), 121-132 DOI: 10.1108/09696479910270452.

Ludwig, C. (1983). *Ludwig's Handbook of New Testament Rulers and Cities.* Denver, CO: Accent Publications Inc.

Madichie, N. (2011). The Darfur Conflict – Geography or Institutions? *Management Decision*, 49(7), 1214-1216.

Malina, B. J., & Rohrbaugh, R. L. (1992). *Social Science Commentary on the Synoptic Gospels* (Kindle ed.). Minneapolis: Fortress Press.

Marquardt, M. J., & Berger, N. O. (2000). *Global Leaders for the 21st Century* . Albany: State University of New York Press.

Marren, P. (2010). Nailing Strategic Jello to the Wall. *Journal of Business Strategy*, 31(3), 59 - 61 DOI: 10.1108/02756661011036727.

Maslach, C., & Leiter, M. (1997). *The Truth About Burnout: How Organizations Cause Personal Stress and What To Do About It.* San Francisco: Jossey-Bass.

Mason, J. (1993). *You're Born an Orginal Don''t Die a Copy.* Tulsa, OK: Insight International.

Maxwell, J. C. (2002). *The Maxwell Leadership Bible.* Nashviile: Thomas Nelson.

May, S. (Ed.). (2012). *Case Studies in Organizational Communication: Ethical Perspectives and Practices* (2 ed.). Thousand Oaks: SAGE Publications, Inc .

McCall Jr., M. W., & Hollenbeck, G. P. (2002). *Developing Global Executives* . Boston: Harvard Business School Publishing.

McEntire, L. E., & Greene-Shortridge, T. M. (2011). Recruiting and Selecting Leaders for Innovation: How to Find the Right Leader. *Advances in Developing Human Resources*(13), 266- 278.

McKinney, M. (2011). *Choosing Service Over Self-Interest: The Focus of Leadership.* Retrieved January 10, 2014, from http://www.leadershipnow.com/service.html

McNeilly, M. (1996). *Sun Tzu and the Art of Business.* New York: Oxford University Press.

Merriam-Webster.com. (2011). Retrieved July 23, 2011, from http://www.merriam-webster.com/dictionary/style

Michaelson, G. A. (2001). *The Art of War for Managers: 50 Strategic Rules.* Avon: Adams Media Corporation.

Miller, C. (1995). *The Empowered Leader.* Nashville, TN: Broadman & Holman Publishers.

Mills, D. (1991). Word Wealth. In *Spirit Filled Life Bible* (p. 1624). Nashville: Thomas Nelson.

Mintzberg, H. (1994). *Rise and Fall of Strategic Planning* . New York: Free Press.

Mintzberg, H., Ahlstrand, B., & Lampel, J. (2005). *Strategy Safari: A Guided Tour Through the Wilds of Strategic Management.* New York: Free Press.

Mitleton-Kelly, E. (2013). *What are the Characteristics of a Learning Organization?* Retrieved from GEMI Metrics Navigator: http://www.gemi.org/metricsnavigator/eag/What%20are%20the%20Characteristics%20of%20a%20Learning%20Organization.pdf

Morden, T. (1999). Models of National Culture—A Management Review. *Cross Cultural Management: An International Journal,* 6(1), 19-44 DOI: 10.1108/13527609910796915.

Morgan, G. (1997). *Images of Organization* (2nd ed.). Thousand Oaks, CA: Sage Publications Inc.

Morrison, T., & Conaway, W. A. (2006). *Kiss, Bow or Shake Hands*. Avon, MA: Adams Media.

Mumford, M. D., Scott, G. M., Gaddis, B., & Strange, J. M. (2002). Leading Creative People: Orchestrating Expertise and Relationships. *The Leadership Quarterly*(13), 705 – 750.

Nadler, D. A., & Tushman, M. L. (1997). *Competing by Design: The Power of Organizational Architecture*. New York: Oxford University Press.

New Media Consortium. (2012). *Horizon Report: 2012 Higher Education Edition*. Retrieved October 31, 2013, from http://www.nmc.org/system/files/pubs/1328995195/2012-Horizon-Report-HE.pdf

Noebel, D. (2006). *Understanding the Times*. Manitou Springs: Summit Ministries (Kindle Edition).

Northouse, P. G. (2007). *Leadership Theory and Practice* (4th ed.). Thousand Oaks, CA: Sage Publications, Inc.

Oguz, F., & Sengün, A. E. (2011). Mystery of the Unknown: Revisiting Tacit Knowledge in the Organizational Literature. *Journal of Knowledge Management*, 15(3), 445-461 DOI: 10.1108/13673271111137420.

Olivares, O. J. (2011). The Formative Capacity of Momentous Events and Leadership Development. *Leadership & Organization Development Journal*, 32(8), 837-853 DOI: 10.1108/01437731111183766.

Oliver, R. W. (1999). Real Time Strategy: Strategy as Sports! War!... Food? *Journal of Business Strategy*, 20(5), 8 - 10 DOI: 10.1108/eb040022 .

O'Neil, J. R. (1993). *The Paradox of Success: A Book of Renewal for Leaders*. New York: Penguin Putnam Books.

Oster, G. W. (2011). *The Light Prize: Perspectives on Christian Innovation*. Virginia Beach, VA: Positive Signs Media.

Palaima, T., & Skaržauskiene, A. (2010). Systems Thinking as a Platform for Leadership Performance in a Complex World. *Baltic Journal of Management*, 5(3), 330-355 DOI: 10.1108/17465261011079749.

Parsons, D. (2007). *Release Your Words: Impact Your World*. Panama City: Parsons Publishing House.

Parsons, D. (2012). *Why Do I Do the Things I Do?* Stafford: Parsons Publishing House.

Pepitone, J. (2011). *CNN Money*. Retrieved October 6, 2013, from http://money.cnn.com/2011/12/15/technology/amazon_kindle_sales/index.htm

Peters, T. (1978). *Futures: Human and Divine.* Atlanta: John Knox Press.

Pfeffer, J. (1998). *The Human Equation Buiding Profits by Putting People First.* Boston: Harvard Business School Press.

Pillemer, D. B.-1. (2011). Pillemer, D. B. *Momentous Events in the Life Story*, 5, 122-134.

Pisapia, J., Reyes-Guerra, D., & Coukos-Semmel, E. (2005). Developing the Leader's Strategic Mindset: Establishing the Measures. Kravis *Leadership Institute, Leadership Review,* 5(Spring), 41-68.

Puryear, E. F. (2002). *American Generalship- Character is Everything: The Art of Command.* Novato, CA: Presidio Press Inc.

Rath, T. (2007). *Strengths Finder 2.0.* New York: Gallup Press.

Raugust, K. (2011). *Publishers Weekly*. Retrieved October 10, 2013, from http://www.publishersweekly.com/pw/by-topic/childrens/childrens-industry-news/article/46267-toy-fair-2010-number-of-publishers-declines-but-children--s-books-still-have-presence.html

Rausch, E. (1996). Guidelines for Participation in Appropriate Decision Making. *Management Development Review*, 9(4), 29-34 DOI: 10.1108/09622519610123751.

Relative, S. (2008). Retrieved July 9, 2013, from http://voices.yahoo.com/fly-like-eagle-steve-miller-band-song-all-865301.html?cat=33

Robbins, V. K. (1996). *Exploring the Texture of Texts A Guide to Socio-Rhetorical Interpretation.* Harrisburg: Trinity Press International.

Rodica, M. B. (2009). The Balanced Scorecard In A Strategy-Focused Organization. *Romania Proceedings* (pp. 79-89). Thessaloniki, Greece: Association of Economic Universities of South and Eastern Europe and the Black Sea Region.

Rorty, R. (1989). *Contingency, Irony, and Solidarity.* Cambridge: Cambridge University Press.

Rorty, R. (1999). *Philosophy and Social Hope.* London: Penguin Books.

Rothwell, W. J. (2005). *Effective Succession Planning 3rd Edition: Ensuring Leadership Continuity and Building Talent from Within.* New York: American Management Association.

Sanchez-Bueno, M. J., & Suarez-Gonzalez, I. (2010). Towards New Organizational Forms. *International Journal of Organizational Analysis,* 18(3), 340 - 357 DOI: 10.1108/19348831011062166.

Sanders, J. T. (2001). When Sacred Canopies Collide: The Reception of the Torah of Moses in the Wisdom Literature of the Second-Temple Period. *Journal for the Study of Judaism*, 32(4), 121-136.

Sanders, T. I. (1998). *Strategic Thinking and the New Science: Planning in the Midst of Chaos, Complexity and Change.* New York: The Free Press.

Schaeffer, F. (1982). Christian Faith and Human Rights. *Simon Greenleaf Law Review*, 2(5), 5.

Schein, E. H. (1997). *Organizational Culture and Leadership* (2nd ed.). San Francisco: Jossey-Bass Inc.

Schneider, J., & Littrell, R. F. (2003). Leadership Preferences of German and English Managers. *Journal of Management Development*, 22(2), 130-148 DOI: 10.1108/02621710310459694.

Schwarzkopf, H. N. (1992). *The Autobiography: It Doesn't Take a Hero.* New York: Bantam Books.

sec.gov. (2010). Retrieved June 7, 2014, from http://www.sec.gov/Archives/edgar/data/1001039/000119312510268910/d10k.htm.

Seidler-de Alwis, R., & Evi, H. (2008). The Use of Tacit Knowledge within Innovative Companies: Knowledge Management in Innovative Enterprises. *Journal of Knowledge Management*, 12(1), 133-147 DOI: 10.1108/13673270810852449.

Sendjaya, S., & Pekerti, A. (2010). Servant leadership as antecedent of trust in organizations. *Leadership & Organization Development Journal*, 643-663.

Severson, K. (2012, July 26). Chick-fil-A Thrust Back Into Spotlight On Gay Rights. *New York Times*, p. 13.

Shahin, A. I., & Wright, P. L. (2004). Leadership in the Context of Culture: an Egyptian Perspective. *Leadership & Organization Development Journal*, 25(6), 499-511 DOI:10.1108/01437730410556743.

Shamir, B., & Eilam, G. (2005). What's your story? A Life-Stories Approach to Authentic Leadership Development. *The Leadership Quarterly*, 16(3), 395-417.

Shillington, G. (2002). *Reading the Sacred Text: An Introduction to Biblical Studies.* New York: The Continuum International Publishing Group Ltd.

Simons, T. L. (1999). Behavioral Integrity as a Critical Ingredient for Transformational Leadership. *Journal of Organizational Change Management*, 12(2), 89-104 DOI: 10.1108/09534819910263640.

Slaughter, R. (1993). Futures Concepts. *Futures*, 25(3), 289-314.

Smith, D. (2001). *The Quotable Walt Disney.* New York: Disney Editions.

Spirit Filled Life Bible (NKJV). (1991). Nashville, TN: Thomas Nelson, Inc.

St. Timothy's Church. (2007). Retrieved July 6, 2011, from http://www.sttimsrome.org/saintwho/saintwho.htm

Stone, A. G., Russell, R. F., & Patterson, K. (2004). Transformational Versus Servant Leadership: A Difference in Leader Focus. *Leadership & Organization Development Journal,* 25(4), 349-361 DOI: 10.1108/01437730410538671.

Strategic Direction. (2008). Innovation is More Than Just a Good Idea: Creative Thinking + Strategic Leadership=Results. *Strategic Direction,* 24(8), 25-27 DOI: 10.1108/02580540810884638.

Strong, J. (1981). *The Exhaustive Concordance of the Bible.* McLean: Macdonald Publishing Company.

Szent-Gyorgyi, A. (1962). *QuotationsPage.com*. Retrieved August 20, 2013, from http://www.quotationspage.com/quotes/Albert_Szent-Gyorgyi/

Tabernero, C., Chambel, M. J., Curral, L., & Arana, J. M. (2009). The Role of Task-Oriented Versus Relationship-Oriented Leadership on Normative Contract and Group Performance. *Social Behavior and Personality: An International Journal,* 37(10), 1391-1404.

Taylor III, B. W. (1996). *Introduction to Management Science*. Saddle River: Prentice Hall.

Thayer, J. H. (1983). *Greek-English Lexicon of the New Testament.* Grand Rapids, MI: Baker Book House.

The Denma Translation Group. (2003). *Sun Tzu: The Art of War.* Boston: Shambhala Publications Inc.

The Executive Fast Track. (2012). Retrieved November 1, 2012, from http://www.12manage.com/methods_mintzberg_ten_schools_of_thought.html

The Hindu. (2011, July 31). Retrieved August 1, 2011, from http://www.thehindu.com/news/national/article2311046.ece

The Strategy Institute of the Boston Consulting Group. (2001). *Clausewitz on Strategy*. (T. von Ghyczy, B. von Oetinger, & C. Bassford, Eds.) New York: John Wiley and Sons.

Thomas, B. (1994). *Walt Disney: An American Original.* New York: Disney Editions.

Tushman, M., & O'Reilly, C. (2002). *Winning through Innovation: A Practical Guide to Leading Organizational Change and Renewal.* Boston: Harvard University School Press.

U.S. Congress. (1996). *Defense of Marriage Act*. Retrieved August 4, 2012, from http://www.govtrack.us/congress/bills/104/hr3396

Ulrich, D., & Ulrich, W. (2010). Creating Abundance. *Leadership Excellence*, 27(6), 8-9.

United Nations. (2006, June). *Support For the Formulation of National Sustainable Development Strategies in Pacific Small Island Developing States*. Retrieved January 21, 2012, from http://www.un.org/esa/sustdev/natlinfo/nsds/pacific_sids/solomon_islands.pdf

Utterback, J. (1996). *Mastering the Dynamics of Innovation*. Boston: Harvard University School Press..

Vaitheeswaran, V. (2008). Innovation is More Than Just a Good Idea: Creative Thinking + Strategic Leadership=Results. *Strategic Direction*, 24(8), 25-27 DOI: 10.1108/02580540810884638.

van Woerkum, C., Aarts, M., & de Grip, K. (2007). Creativity, Planning and Organizational Change. *Journal of Organizational Change Management*, 20(6), 847-865 DOI: 10.1108/09534810710831055.

Vanderpyl, T. (2012). Rest is the Hidden Key to Successful Leadership. *Human Resource Management International Digest*, 20(7), 3-4.

Vine, W. (1985). *Expository Dictionary Of New Testament Words*. McLean: Macdonald Publishing Company.

Von Krogh, G., Ichijo, K., & Nonaka, I. (2000). *Enabling Knowledge Creation: How to Unlock the Mystery of Tacit Knowledge and Release the Power of Innovation*. Oxford: Oxford Press.

Washington, G. (1789). *The American Presidency Project*. (J. T. Woolley, & G. Peters, Editors) Retrieved February 25, 2012, from http://www.presidency.ucsb.edu/ws/?pid=25800

Watson, R. (2012). *Future Files: A Brief History of the Next 50 Years. Boston*: Nicholas Brealey Publishing.

Wigram, G. (1979). *The Englishman's Greek Concordance*. Grand Rapids, MI: Baker Book House.

Willard, D. (2002). *Renovation of the Heart: Putting on the Character of Christ*. Colorado Springs: NavPress.

Winston, B. (2002). *Be A Leader for God's Sake*. Virginia Beach: School of Global Leadership & Entrepreneurship.

Winston, B. E., & Patterson, K. (2006). An Integrative Definition of Leadership. *International Journal of Leadership Studies*, 1(2), 6-66.

Woll, T. (2002). *Publishing for Profit.* Chicago: Chicago Review Press.

Woolfe, L. (2002). *The Bible on Leadership : From Moses to Matthew Management Lessons for Contemporary Leaders.* New York: American Management Association.

World Vision. (2012). Retrieved November 12, 2012, from http://www.worldvision.org/content.nsf/about/history

Wren, D. A., & Bedeian, A. G. (2009). *The Evolution of Management Thought* (6th ed.). Hoboken, NJ: John Wiley & Sons, Inc.

Wright, N. T. (Director). (1998). *Jesus the New Way Video Series* [Motion Picture].

Wright, N. T. (1999). *The Challenge of Jesus.* Downers Grove: InterVarsity Press.

Wuellner, F. S. (1998). *Feed My Shepherds: Spiritual Healing and Renwal for Those in Christian Leadership.* Nashville: Upper Room Books .

Yaprak, A., & Sheldon, K. T. (1984). Political Risk Management in Multinational Firms: An Integrative Approach. *Management Decision,* 22(6), 53.

Yukl, G. A. (2009). *Leadership in Organizations* (7 ed.). Englewood Cliffs, NJ: Prentice Hall.

Zachary, L. J. (2005). *Creating a Mentoring Culture: The Organization's Guide.* San Francisco: Emerald Group Publishing.

Zhang, Y., Goonetilleke, R. S., Plocher, T., & Liang, S.-F. M. (2004). *Time Orientation and Human Performance.* Hong Kong: Work with Computing Systems 2004 (Proceedings of the 7th International Conference).

Zweifel, T. D. (2003). *Culture Clash: Managing the Global High-Performance Team.* New York: Swiss Consulting Group Inc.

MORE BOOKS BY DR. DARRELL PARSONS

EMERGING AS AN INNOVATIVE LEADER

12 Common Cores for Mobilizing Your Influence into the Future

by Dr. Darrell J. Parsons

Out of the dust of failing organizations or fresh out of the halls of academia, a new breed of leader is emerging to take the reigns in our world, in our politics, and in our families. Do you have the skillset you need to propel you into the the forefront of your world? From out of the myriad of research, Darrell Parsons is able to concisely articulate twelve of the most important competencies which are imperative for today's innovative leader. Trustworthiness is an excellent characteristic to develop in all aspects of your life; however, how does a leader utilize trust in his cohort to add value to the organization? Also included in the common core is ethics, context, leadership succession, and understanding people. Innovate your life today! Available in hardback, $24.95. Also, available in e-book formats.

WHY DO I DO THE THINGS I DO?

Understanding Personalities

by Darrell J. Parsons

In this insightful book, Darrell Parsons identifies the four primary types of personalities and how they interact together. As you grow in understanding, you will gain the tools you need for developing successful relationships in all areas of your life. Available in trade paper, $10.95. Also, available in e-book formats.